Track It
to
Crack It

Track It
to
Crack It

The Ultimate Guide to Unlocking Your Company's Full Potential

Susan Raisanen

On the Inside Press
Beverly Hills, CA 90210

Track It to Crack It: The Ultimate Guide to Unlocking Your Company's Full
Potential

Copyright © 2015 by Susan Raisanen
www.ProfitFinderPro.com

Published by On the Inside Press
Beverly Hills, CA 90210
www.OntheInsidePress.com

Library of Congress Control Number 2014956468
ISBN 978-0-9829153-2-5 Print
ISBN 978-1-943280-51-3 eBook

Cover design by Carli Smith.

Printed in the United States of America.

With love and gratefulness to Mom and Dad.

Home is where this story began.

Thank you to my brothers and sisters,
whose invaluable recollections helped fill out this book.

Special thanks to my brothers,
Warren and Randy,
who read through every word and helped me refine my message.

Table of Contents

Foreword

One of my favorite authors and thought leaders, C.S. Lewis, said, "Courage is not simply one of the virtues, but the form of every virtue at the testing point." These were wise words that I liken unto my own expression that, "Tracking is not simply one of business' best practices, but the form of every business best practice at the testing point."

As the former CEO of Guerrilla Marketing, I could rattle off hundreds of guerrilla marketing weapons that I or Jay Conrad Levinson have come up with, but without tracking you are just shooting in the dark.

Every business owner, marketing leader, or sales executive must know that marketing is measuring...and as Peter Drucker would say, "What gets measured gets improved."

Real businesses spend money on sales, marketing, advertising, and man power to be profitable. Really great businesses track all of these things, knowing where their time and resources are best spent. If you are lucky your new business might be succeeding despite not following these laws of the business universe, but luck runs out eventually.

If you don't want to rely on luck and you want to invest in what works, you must track it to crack it. Susan Raisanen, an executive with a knack for the numbers, is about to show you just that. Pay attention closely because she has a track record for magnifying profits for people.

In this easy to read, example-rich book you will learn the numbers that matter most, how to find them, follow them, and improve them without spending a lot of time. Susan comes from a long line of entrepreneurs, business experts, and trackers.

This once school teacher and principal turned entrepreneur and software executive is guaranteed to make complex things simple in this book. Even if you started tracking half your business, you might double your profits! So Enjoy.

David Fagan
CEO, Icon Builder Media

Introduction

Is a Good Night's Sleep Only a Dream?

Imagine you went into work in the morning feeling refreshed after having spent some good, fun time with your family the evening before, laughing and visiting and doing the things that families do, getting some exercise, eating a nice meal, and then ending the day with a good night's sleep. When you woke in the morning, it was probably pretty easy to jump out of bed, and somehow everything felt right; you were able to start the day with a smile.

This kind of person is really fun to be around, right? They just always seem so positive, their enthusiasm and zest for life is catchy, and before you know it, you are smiling, too.

Unfortunately, we all know the other kind of person as well. The Grouch. Have you ever been on the way to work and found yourself wondering what kind of mood So-and-So would be in today? Wondering whether or not you would have to steer clear? Would Grouch be stressed out again, rushing in at the last minute or even late, morose or in a foul mood? The one whose cloud weighs you down, too?

Look at yourself. How are you going into work each day? Are you the excited and enthused person, or The Grouch? If you are the first, great. Look at what you are doing and keep it up!

> Sleep has become a foreign concept for some small business owners.

Unfortunately, many business owners and managers fall under The Grouch category, and part of the reason is because sleep has become a foreign concept, especially

1

when there are pressing issues at work that weigh on their minds. Their stressed minds and thoughts are still spinning at 2:00, 3:00, and 4:00 in the morning when they should be shut down and at rest.

Enough research has proven that we need a certain amount of sleep each night in order for our body to do its work to restore, repair, and rejuvenate itself. The brain even has specific rejuvenating functions that occur during sleep, so after a good night's rest we waken with a fresher, clearer mind, and our entire perspective on life looks much better.

Stress is a killer because it deprives us of sleep. When a person does not get sleep, the body gets inflamed. This allows the immune system to break down, and illness sets in. We humans cannot operate without sleep for too long. Eventually something gives: the family, the body or the mind.

So what is it that is keeping you up at night?

According to some recent surveys I read, four of the top five reasons for staying awake are repeated across questionnaires, although not necessarily in the same order.

1. How can I get more customers (generate new sales) and keep the ones I already have?
2. How can I keep expenses from eating my profits?
3. How can I keep a positive cash flow?
4. How can I grow my business?

There are other issues, too, but these are four that came across repeatedly through several different reports (*The Business News Daily* June 2013, *Fox Business* June 2013, *Baylor Business Review* FA11)

If these same questions keep you awake at night, you are not alone. In fact, there are hundreds and thousands of others that are pondering the same questions, turning the same thoughts, and losing the same sleep.

We were there, too, until we figured out that we needed to make some changes to ease the mind and help us in our businesses. In turn, this had a domino effect all the way down the line.

One thing is certain, and that is, if you want to change the direction of your business, you need to make some changes in the way you do things. This does not mean the changes have to be big or complicated, but there has to be some meaningful change in regards to the profit-making points of your business.

My focus in this book is especially on certain strategies in the sales and marketing end of your business that, if implemented, will help answer and alleviate a lot of the stress of the four questions, some through direct association and others through indirect association. These are strategies that worked for us, and may work for you, too, so take from it what you can. Even small tweaks to the way you do things can make a big difference.

Wouldn't it be fun to be able to enjoy your business more and have fun working on operating profitably and growing instead of always having to be working on casualty prevention? How would a little stress relief help your life at the office and at home?

Chapter 1

Tracking Says it All

Business owners are great at making decisions. One of Napoleon Hill's Laws of Success is the ability to make quick decisions and change them slowly. In leadership and business we add to that and say that the decisions they make, however, can only be as good as the information they have!

So how do you get that information? You track!

Let me explain why tracking is so important to me. I came by it honestly, and it was pretty much a learned behavior. I grew up in a big family on a working dairy farm in Minnesota. My parents tracked everything! As a kid I knew all those lists and records were needed in order to know and have certain information on hand, but it was not until many years later that I realized how it all fit into running a business, even the business of a dairy farmer.

One morning when I had just begun writing this book, I was thinking back and remembering different things about life on the farm, both in the house and in the barn and fields. As I started thinking of the things Dad tracked, the list started formulating. After a few minutes, it was quite long. I was so excited that I called my brother, and reminisced on all the things that Dad kept track of. We had really been tracking all our lives. I'll tell you more about that later, but let's talk about why tracking should be important to you.

Tim was a roofing business owner in Tennessee. He had a small business and wanted to take that to a whole new level. If he could get systems in place that worked, and repeat the processes over and over again, he could grow, and not only grow, but grow profitably.

He started by tracking his leads. Long story short, within 25 months that $2.5 million business grew to $12.5 million. I asked him what he did, and he said that he had started tracking. The first thing he noticed was that he was not a very good salesman. He needed to get out of his own way, so he hired more salespeople. Then Mother Nature helped out with some storms for that year, so he was able to get really good business out of that. However, even after all the storms had calmed down, since he had his systems in place, he was able to gain the market share in that area. The following year, they were on track for $8.5 million. So whether he was going from $2.5 to $12.5 million or $2.5 to $8.5 million, that is a big jump in just a few years.

> *W*ithin 25 months of his tracking start, his business went from $2.5 million to $12.5 million.

Business owners who have successfully grown their businesses have put systems into place *in order* to grow, not *after* they have grown! They are proactive and taking steps to grow intentionally.

Consider all the successful people around you, or the successful business owners you have read about. All of those businesses in the Big 500 have all their statistics readily available, the very numbers that measure and prove their success.

Darren Hardy, author of *The Compound Effect*, says, "All winners are trackers. Right now I want you to track your life with the same intention: to bring your goals within sight."

Think about your weight. If you are in good physical shape and at a healthy weight, you probably are one to step on the scale somewhat regularly, and you know within a few pounds of what you weigh. You monitor those numbers, and if they start fluctuating too much, you adjust your activity and food intake. If you are overweight, you probably do not get on the scale as often as you should, maybe even seldom, if ever. You do not really know for sure what you weigh, and your weight probably keeps going up. You shrug your shoulders in dismay and say that you really do not eat that much, and it seems like you get adequate exercise; however, if you were to go on some sort of fitness plan, and begin to track and adjust your intake and output, the weight would probably disappear.

Consider the pros in every sport! Every hit they ever made and every ball they ever threw has numbers attached to it and is verifiable in the records. They and their fans know the running numbers of RBIs, goals made, throws tossed, penalties, and so on. Their moves are tracked, measured and recorded on a game-by-game basis.

If you are a golfer, you track your golf scores. You track the pitch of the golf course and what club you need to use to get that little white ball to go where you want it to go. The surface of the ground makes a difference. The direction and speed of the wind all factor into your decisions on how to hit. The distance from your fairway placement to the green determines which iron you use. Many different factors play into a golf score, and the one who has paid the closest attention to the details has a better score than the one who just goes out and randomly whacks at the ball.

In *Moneyball*, Billy Beane, the former pro baseball player who became the general manager of the Oakland A's, changed the game of scouting forever after the work he did through hiring based on numbers! He needed to put together a competitive team with a limited payroll. He used all the little numbers and statistics to isolate and quantify where a player was good, and then built his team that way. Doing so, Billy Beane ended up having a Major League winning team for consecutive years.

How about balancing your checking or debit account? Growing your savings account? If you want it to grow, you are going to watch it, make the calculations, and adjust your spending and earnings and investments, as necessary.

The exact same holds true in business. According to McKinsey & Company's DataMatics 2013 survey of more than 400 top managers of large international companies from a wide variety of industries, companies that track and use customer analytics and intelligence are 6.5 times more likely to retain customers, 7.4 times more likely to outperform their competitors on making sales to existing customers, and *nearly 19 times* more likely to achieve above-average profitability. (Louis Columbus, *Forbes* Contributing Editor, July 14, 2014)

According to the same survey, the senior management, in whatever capacity that may be, whether it's a business owner, CEO, or president, must value and take action on the intelligence or data of its company, and make sure that the intelligence is part of the strategy of the business, the part that drives the decisions. Customer analytics and its use are all driven by the leadership of the company, and leadership that expects fact-based decisions which then convert to actions with measurable results are the leaders and companies that win. This will differentiate the high performers from the slackers. (McKinsey & Company's DataMatics 2013 survey, January 2014)

Granted, these results were from large companies, but they did not get large on accident. There is an old saying that most successful business people know and embrace: *If you can't measure it, you can't manage it.*

Whether your goals be personal or professional, the only sure way to make progress is to know where you have been, where you are going and what happens along the way.

Have you ever run a lemonade stand or helped a child run one? In my little Midwest hometown, we have a Corn Carnival every August. During that same week there are citywide garage sales. Without a doubt, there are also many of those little entrepreneurs-in-the-making selling lemonade and cookies on the curb.

I asked one little girl if they were making some pretty good money. She told me that she did not know yet because she had to count all their expenses. They would need to pay their mom for the costs first, and then they could count the profits. Their expenses included the supplies for making the signs and the ingredients for the lemonade and cookies. After they counted all that, they would know the profits. They had a little notebook and wrote down every sale, what it was, and who made the sale.

In talking with their mother, I asked if she noticed a difference in the salesmanship of the different kids. "Yes," she said. One was hollering and waving in customers down at the street corner and chatting up the customers while the next would pretty much just mind his own business quietly at the stand and, if someone happened to walk up to him, he would make a sale.

At the end of the day, these kids counted their money, and they were so excited about their profits that they re-invested that money back into more ingredients for the next day. Do you think they were going to double their profits? They sure figured so.

Look at this example a little closer. These little kids (salespeople) were using ingredients (expenses) to make cookies and lemonade (products). Each child (salesperson) was paid (commissions) according to how they got business (marketing) to come to their stand and buy (sales).

After subtracting expenses (cost of sale) from their sales (gross revenues), they used the remaining money (profits) to reinvest in their business to grow it even bigger and make more the next day, planning on larger profits at the end (forecasting).

What did you think of the way the one child was selling compared to the other one? The advertising seemed to be working for her. So would not you as a parent (sales manager) go to the next one and suggest that since standing on the corner is working for this child, maybe you could go stand on that corner?

> *Your business is no different than a lemonade stand, just on a larger scale.*

Your business is no different. It is just on a larger scale!

Questions for Your Business:

1. What were your gross revenues last year? Last quarter? Last month?
2. What would you like your gross revenues to be next year? Next quarter? Next month?
3. What specific steps have you taken to make sure you are on track for reaching those goals?
4. How are you measuring your benchmarks?

NOTES

_____

_____

_____

_____

_____

_____

_____

_____

_____

_____

_____

_____

_____

_____

Chapter 2

Unlocking Your Numbers

Did you start your business because you were good at doing *Something*, and then you decided to turn that *Something* into a business? Congratulations! That is wonderful, and it says a lot about you. You are a person who has the guts and gumption to take some risk, and that category is reserved for only a very special type of person.

Most entrepreneurs started this way. This also means, as the business owner, you now wear all kinds of hats; a hat for sales, marketing, accounting and fulfillment. All the responsibilities of the business have fallen straight on your shoulders, at least for the moment.

Let's say that you have started your business, and have been operating a few years. You have brought on some salespeople, and you are actively spending money on marketing. You sort of have an idea of how things should run in your business, but in a very broad sense. Now you want to take it to the next level, so somehow you need to ramp it up and start growing. Where do you start?

The challenging part here comes up in a couple ways. First of all, people opening a new business for the first time have not necessarily attended a formal business school, and have not had the experiences in that particular School of Hard Knocks yet. Just because a person is good at doing *Something* does not mean they understand everything that goes into running a business: sales, marketing, accounting, training, and managing. There is a definite learning curve, and the sooner it can be learned, the better for the business.

Second, there are only 24 hours in a day. As new business owners, the business is usually understaffed and overworked. Maybe it is even a one-man band with that one man wearing every hat. Time and time management becomes an issue. Where is a person's time best spent?

Well, it seems the time best spent would be on the profit points of your business. Where is that? How do you know what to watch? How do you know what to manage?

You start by tracking. Where are you now? Where are you going? What are the steps along the way?

If your phone is ringing, you have probably been spending some money on advertising and have a sense that something is working because the phone is ringing. However, as the number of dollars spent increases, a nagging thought starts lingering in the back of your mind. "I wonder which advertising is *really* bringing in the phone calls." Knowing that some is working and some is not, you quickly become familiar with the adage which has been tied to merchants as far back as 1860, and the founder of the first department store, John Wanamaker, that "fifty percent of my marketing works. I just don't know which fifty percent," Who coined the phrase originally, who knows? That does not matter. What matters is that the same issue business owners faced almost a couple hundred years ago is sometimes still a real dilemma for business owners today.

Have you ever had that gnawing in your gut as someone sits before you and gives an offer to do more marketing for you? They ask the stupid question, "Do you want to grow your business or not?" Sometimes I wonder what they would say if I answered, 'No, I'd prefer to just sink my business right into the ground.' That is kind of an annoying question, isn't it? The thing is, they have you in a Catch-22, and they know they are messing with your mind! Your brain tells you that you have to market, yet your gut tells you that you are sick and tired of spending money and not knowing whether or not it is working.

This is the position we were in before we decided we needed to change. We were spending a lot of money on marketing and had all kinds of salespeople, but we had no way to measure who was selling what, nor did we know what the cost was to us per salesperson, per advertising source and per service and product we offered. We knew that if we had this information, we could make better decisions with our marketing and sales departments, and so we set out to tie it all together.

The starting point for us was to track our leads, sales, and marketing. In turn, it answered these four questions:

1. How can I get more customers (generate new sales) and keep the ones I already have?
2. How can I keep expenses from eating my profits?
3. How can I keep a positive cash flow?
4. How can I grow my business?

And that made all the difference.

To demonstrate my point a little more clearly, let's look at Ryan's company.

Ryan and his brother, Ken, have had a gutter business for about 15 years in Poughkeepsie, NY. Ryan always kept good records, but he did not really know how to use all the numbers he had gathered. He said he was sick of "just making" payroll each week, and knew there was a way to get around that to even out the cash flow. It was not until they hired a business coach who was pretty savvy with numbers, however, that Ryan was able to pull his mind around the numbers and put them in an order that made sense.

This particular company needed to do some price adjustments, and they were having a hard time justifying the increase in their minds; but when they looked at the numbers, they had to do what made sense for the company. They had to take a look at the industry as a whole to see what could be charged. They also had to determine their own gross margins to make sure that it was profitable for them. Then they had to really outshine their competition in both service and quality in order to justify their increase. It was a mind game for Ryan, and in the end he said he just had to "let the numbers decide". For him, that has taken away a lot of what can cause anxiety in running a business.

Since they know their average close rate, based on the number of leads, Ryan is able to predict the number and dollars of sales, as well as the timeline for delivering on those sales. In their company, they want a turnaround time of two weeks to deliver on a sale. If he sees that there are a certain number of leads in Week 1, he knows that in Week 2 he will have a certain number of sales, which will mean a certain number of jobs for Weeks 3 and 4. Knowing the number of jobs each crew can complete in a week, he is able to plan the number of crews that will be needed to deliver on time for all of those sales. He also knows and can plan for the approximate cash flow that will come upon projected completion times of gutter installations.

Another way that tracking has helped them is by mapping out the lag times. Their business is seasonal, and there is a drop in both sales and production during the winter. Knowing this, they are better able to make more productive use of their time during the busy season. Because of history, he knows approximately how many crews he will need during each month. If he has six people out on the roads in March, but knows that in April he has

> *Tracking helped map out their lag times, allowing them to more effectively ramp up crews.*

historically needed ten, he has ample time to ramp up his crews in preparation for when ten are needed.

Now, after having all goals and expectations in place that are driven strictly by the numbers, Ryan said that every person in their company knows exactly what is expected of them on a weekly and monthly basis. There is no more guessing, and all decisions are made based on the numbers. He has embraced the idea that his coach told him, "Employees do not cost you money; they make you money." If or when it turns the other way, then it is time to part ways. Even though those situations are not always easy, decisions that can be so difficult are made much easier when they are driven by the numbers. The decisions are made in the best interest of keeping the business running profitably.

That is part of the beauty of tracking. It keeps you one step ahead of the game, and often two steps ahead of the competition...because in so many cases, your competition is not doing it.

Questions for Your Business:

1. Why did you start your business?
2. Where are the main Profit Points of your business?
3. How much time are you spending on the Profit Points compared to the other tasks?
4. What are you doing to make sure you can focus your attentions on the Profit Points?
5. How do you get new customers while keeping the ones you already have?
6. What specific steps have you taken to keep expenses from eating your profits? How do you measure that?
7. What specific steps have you taken to keep a positive cash flow?
8. What steps are you taking to grow your business profitably?

NOTES

_____

_____

_____

_____

_____

_____

_____

_____

_____

_____

_____

_____

_____

_____

Chapter 3

Where Do I Begin Tracking?

The most fun starts once you have a period of tracking history, whether it be a month or two or three or more. By then you have numbers and data to use to examine, manipulate and change, but initially you have to start at the very beginning.

Your tracking should start from the very moment a customer contacts you with an interest in an estimate or even interest about your business. Whether that new prospect contacted you by phone, email, in person, or online, you should have a way to capture that information so that you have, at a minimum, a phone number and address. Ideally, you will also get an email address, as well. You will use these addresses, phone numbers and email addresses as a way to keep in touch now and in the future.

Usually people will not hand out their contact information just because you want to fill your database, but if you give a reason for needing it, they are happy to give it. For example, if you have a home improvement business, it is obvious that you will need an address to go out to their home to assess the situation and give an estimate. The reason for needing an address then is self-explanatory, and they are happy to give it.

However, if you do not necessarily need to go out to their home, but you have a packet of information you would like to send to them that would help educate them on the service you are providing, let them know that. Most people are willing to give an address as long as what you are sending is legitimate and desirable. For example, you can ask in this way: "I have a great informational booklet that we have put together about pond habitats, and others have really appreciated this information. What is a good mailing address to send this to you?"

The prospect will usually give out their mailing address as long as what you are offering is something that will be of interest and benefit to them. Then once you say you are going to send something make certain that you do! On top of that, make sure that whatever it is you are sending is worth it and gives your prospect and future customer the impression that yes, you are the expert, a professional and your advice and instruction is worth reading.

As for email addresses, if you have that booklet or information in PDF format or digitized, it is legitimate to ask for an email address in order to send it that way, too. On the other hand, keep in mind that sometimes it is okay to not have something desirable available in digital format, because then it gives a reason to get both snail mail and email addresses.

> Once you say you're going to send them something of value, make sure you do!

I have found that a great way to legitimately ask for an email address is to send appointment confirmations that way. Once you have booked an appointment, ask them, 'Would you like me to send you an appointment confirmation by email?' Do not bother asking if they have email; just ask if you can send them an appointment confirmation. People who use email will usually be happy to get a confirmation email. According to the records of one of the companies I work with, about eight out of ten give their email address.

Every once in a while, someone may hesitate or ask if you sell or give out your list or if you are going to send them all kinds of junk mail. First of all, tell them your intentions and how you plan to use their email address. I recommend telling them you will never sell or give your list to others, and then stick to that. If you send a monthly newsletter, let them know. If you plan to send notifications of specials you are running, let them know. Let them also know that they can be removed from the list if they do not want to get your mail. Second, do not abuse your permission to use their email by sending all kinds of junk mail.

It usually is not an issue to get someone's email address, but again it depends on why you need or want it. Make that reason legitimate and beneficial to the prospect.

If you have web forms that people fill out and submit to your office, try to get as much information as you can without going overboard. Again, it has to be a legitimate reason to request the information. One web developer I worked with told me that anything more than an email address is too much to ask. Another said the main thing to get is a phone number. That is not necessarily true; it depends on the person and the industry. Some prefer phone calls to emails, or vice versa. Give them the option of either or both.

For example, one company I'm involved with has absolutely no problem getting a name, mailing address, phone number, email address, reason for request, how they heard about the company, the type of service they are requesting and the best time to notify them. That is because the information asked there was all legitimate, with the exception of how they heard about the company. But that was inserted in the form in a quick dropdown with predetermined options, including a text box for 'other'. People had absolutely no hesitations in filling it out, even though the fields other than first name and phone number were the only required fields.

On the other hand, people who submit requests through another business I am involved with are very hesitant about giving out personal contact information. That is perfectly fine with me, as long as they give at least a phone number to call and make initial contact and speak with them a bit. Once we have started to build a relationship, we usually get the other information. You can be sure that on that very first call, we capture their email addresses. Again, it has to be legitimate and beneficial to the recipient.

Bit by bit, you can build your customer list, depending on the industry you are in, and the type of customers you have. With the use of the internet nowadays, it is easy to find the rest of the contact information if you have even a phone number or email address.

I love whitepages.com. If we have nothing more than a name or phone number, we can often fill in the blanks ourselves, as long as they have a land line or registered cell phone number. It is always worth a try. In fact, just recently one of the businesses I'm associated with did this for someone who called their office. The prospect called in fishing for a little bit of information. When the scheduler asked for his phone number, he said he would talk to his wife (whose name he mentioned), and then call back in a couple weeks. That was not necessarily the desired outcome, but it was fine. After hanging up, the scheduler went to whitepages.com, looked up his name and found it there. She had remembered his wife's name, and that name was associated in the white pages for a man with the same name, so she was quite certain she had the right one.

A little more than two weeks later when this man had not called back, she took the chance and called him. There was no answer, so she left a message, saying who she was, and that when they had spoken a couple weeks ago, he was going to talk to his wife and get back to her to set an appointment. Since he did not get back, she was hoping he had not lost their number and wanted to just touch base to see what day would work for him and his wife to meet with a representative. Guess what? He called back in short order and was so happy she had called. They set a time, and not too long after there was a subsequent sale of tens of thousands of dollars.

Was it worth it for her to pay attention to his name when he gave it over the phone, record it, and spend two minutes looking it up on whitepages.com? Was it worth it to be bold enough to call him? Sometimes people just get tied up and busy in life, so if you can do them the favor of making yourself and your wanted or necessary service easily available, they will appreciate it.

Back to capturing initial lead information.

Now that you have the contact information, next you want at least three other very necessary pieces. These are pieces that are very simple to gather from the conversation you have with them, even if that "conversation" is a web form.

First of all, how did they hear about you? This is very necessary information for you to have; in fact, it is crucial to your sales and marketing success in many ways, which will be explained a little later on.

If you are spending money on marketing and/or handing out your company leads to sales reps and not tracking this, you are losing money. Guaranteed.

While you are talking, just ask them how they heard about you. Just make it an easy part of your conversation. You should be familiar with whatever marketing campaigns you have going at any given time, so that when they tell you, it makes sense. Mark down both paid and unpaid advertising. If leads are coming in through your website, tag your contact pages on the different sites so you know which pages are drawing the internet leads.

Marketing is like a wheel, though, and most companies are advertising in many places, so the wheel has many spokes. There are times when people have heard about you on the radio or have seen your billboard ads or other advertising in a variety of places. That's okay. That means all your touches of marketing are creating an awareness for the prospect to make contact with you.

So in your conversation with them after you ask, 'How'd you hear about us?', and they say, 'I found you on the internet,' it is easy to say something like, 'Oh, had you heard an ad and checked us out or something?' Again, have a dialogue, not just a drilling questionnaire. People would rather visit than just answer questions. Once you have gathered that information, mark down whatever it was that drove them to the website. For the leads that come in online, by having a dropdown of advertising venues on the website, they are more likely to check how they heard about you rather than just saying "on the internet".

We have advertised on several different radio stations. One is with a pretty well-known talk show host, and the other is not as well-known. That conversation is usually easy when they say they heard us on the radio. For one thing, we know the times our ads play, and so we can just ask, 'Oh, good. What station do you usually listen to? (Pay attention in case this is not the station you are on; it will tell you about possibilities for future advertising.)

Or did you hear us on your drive home? Or was it the early morning drive with Mr. Talk Show Host?'

As in most things, there will be some margin of error. They may accidentally say that they heard you on one station instead of the one they really heard you on; however, those overall trends will show and in time the information and patterns will become more dependable.

Now that you marked the lead source, the second piece of information is to tie this lead to a salesperson. Who did you assign the lead to? Just mark it down. If you are giving company leads, you want to have a record of which salesperson was assigned each lead. Simple as that.

And then the third bit of information you definitely want to capture is what service or product they are interested in. Try to come up with maybe four main categories or reasons why people call you, and at least narrow all the calls down to one of the four. If you want to create sub-categories, that is even better, and I highly recommend it. You will see why soon.

By this time you have captured enough information that is necessary for the beginning of good lead, sales and marketing management.

That is not to say there are not other bits and pieces of information you should not have. I recommend taking impeccable notes on every conversation you have with a prospect or customer. It is helpful to even make notes of human interests, conversational pieces and other bits of information that help you to work best with that person. If you found out the person is going on a trip, mark it down. Then the next time you call, even if it is four months later, ask how the trip was. If they are battling some illness or facing some difficulty, mark it down. If they just had a baby, mark it down. If they love sailing, mark it down. If they have gate codes, mark it down. If they hate certain colors, mark it down. Get the idea? Mark it down.

Those notes you took will help you pick up the conversation at a later date. Not only will it help you pick up the conversation, but it will help you remember the person better. We all know that when we speak with many people in one week, we have the best intentions of remembering the entire conversation and are quite certain we will. But, alas and alack! They slip through the cracks. Our brains cannot hold all that information and a lot just slips away. That is exactly why we write it down.

> *T*aking notes on the conversations you have with potential clients will help you remember the conversation and the person better.

If you have someone at the front desk or in scheduling setting the initial appointments with your prospects and customers, ask them to be specific in their notes, too. The more you can have and remember about a person, the easier it is to build relationships. Your customers will be impressed that you remembered certain things about the conversation, and in turn, that translates to "this person listens".

Of course, you also want to write down the appointment times, and keep a running list of when you have had contact or been out to meet with this person. This sounds way too basic, but there are still people who do not do this!

Let me illustrate. I met with the administrator of what appeared to be a successful roofing company. They had quite a few trucks on the road and seemed to be buzzing – from the outside anyhow. Of course, I did not see their Profit and Loss statements, so I do not know the true financial condition of the company.

Anyhow, I asked the administrator to tell me a little about their lead gathering and distribution process. She said that when a phone call came in, the front desk took down the caller's name and number on a sticky note and gave it to a sales rep. That was it. No more.

Needless to say, all I could think about was all the customers, sales, and revenues they were leaving behind.

Hopefully this does not describe your company, but if it does, it is a good thing you are reading this book. Hopefully your eyes and mind will be opened to see how much more you could be making if you embraced tracking.

So now what?

Questions for Your Business:

1. When someone calls your business to set an appointment, what kind of information do you gather?
2. Do you have a gift or some sort of information packet you could send your prospective customers when they set an appointment?
3. How would it benefit you to have someone who would get the customer information and schedules appointments at the time of the call so that your sales reps and the prospective customer do not have to play phone tag?
4. Do you ask how the prospective customers heard about you? Do you have a way to track that in the record?
5. Do your sales reps have easy and quick access to customer records and the appointment calendar?

NOTES

_____

_____

_____

_____

_____

_____

_____

_____

_____

_____

_____

_____

_____

_____

Chapter 4

Lead Count

Once you get leads in, it is helpful for you to be able to see immediately where the leads are coming from and what kind of service or product the people are requesting. This kind of information carries even more meaning once you have a history of tracking, because then you can use the data to make some pretty quick projections based on what has historically taken place.

The information for the lead count does not have to be complicated. All you really need to know for this is where your leads came from, what kind of leads they were, and what they cost. Then tie it together something like this.

July 1-31

Lead Source	Service 1	Service 2	Total Leads	Ad Costs	Ad Cost/ Lead
Radio Station	14	2	16	$7,000	$437.50
Direct Mail	2	9	11	$800	$72.73
Trade Show	57	35	92	$5,000	$54.35
Referrals	15	9	24	$0	$0
Prev. Customers	18	20	38	$0	$0
TOTAL	**106**	**75**	**181**	**$12,800**	**$70.72**

When you look at it laid out like this, you can see that you had 106 leads for Service 1 and 75 leads for Service 2 from the various lead sources, for a total number of 181 leads. Those 181 leads cost you $12,800 or $70.72 per lead. It appears that the trade show was a good one because it brought in 92 leads. The radio is looking questionable because it brought in so few leads, and the cost was quite high. You also have a number of leads from unpaid advertising, or referrals and previous customers, which is good. Whether or not you have enough leads to be profitable from any of these advertising sources is yet to be determined; it depends on the revenues that come in.

This is certainly just a beginning, and no final decisions should be made based on this alone, unless you are paying for advertising that is bringing in *no* leads.

So now to give you the big picture. Once you have established a history of tracking, you will be able to look at the number of leads you received during a certain period of time. Based on the average closing ratio, contract size, and conversion time, you can already make projections based on these numbers.

For example, if you have a window company, and you know that your company's overall average closing ratio is 33% with an average contract of $10,000, from these leads as shown above, you figure you will generate approximately 60 sales for a total of $600,000. Since you have these separated by lead source, you can also use this same method for forecasting sales on each individual lead source. As you will come to know, different lead sources have different close ratios.

You should also know what the average time to convert a lead to a sale is and how long it takes to deliver. If it takes five days to convert, and from there it is about a month before you can deliver on the sale, this means your receipts for these billable sales for approximately $600,000 will start coming into your hands in a little over a month, maybe even five weeks. The exception to this time frame would be down payments. Those should start coming as soon as the leads are converted, so within approximately five days. The number of sales reps you have will determine the length of time before the leads are followed up on and sold.

Based on the number of leads, you can also predict the number of crews or fulfillment teams you will need available within a certain time frame in order to keep your completion of the sales and flow of cash on a steady and predictable stream.

On the other hand, if you have a lull in leads, there will be a lull in sales and production, all lagging one after the other. Since that dip can be forecasted, if you are really on the ball you will have some sort of spiff to offer with a real quick sale and turnaround time to compensate and bring revenues in so that the dip is not so noticeable.

One company comes to mind in thinking of spiffs. When the leads are slow, they send out a Good News/Bad News mass email to their list. The good news is that if anyone is interested in having their home painted, they can be fit in quickly because the painters have some days coming up in the next couple weeks. The bad news is that if the company does not fill the empty days, they may lose their great painters because they won't stay if they're not kept busy. Every single time the company sends out that blast, they get calls for painting. They are truthful because they do see a lull in business, and they are able to do a quick turnaround on painting. Works every time. What kind of quick offer can you come up with that will benefit both you and your customers?

Another way to use the lead count and cost form is for negotiating for different advertising. Most people who have been buying advertising for any amount of time understand the frustration of spending money while not knowing if it is going to work for them. It's a risk, almost like gambling. What if no leads come in? Well, sometimes that happens. The thing is, when you track, it's easier to take calculated risks.

If you are a company that tracks and can show your marketing agencies proof of that, if they are determined to stand behind all the rhetoric and talk of how great their marketing is, they will pay attention. And they may even work with you.

One company with whom I am associated had been spending around $11,000 per month for ads in the Sunday paper for years, and it paid off. It made sense to continue buying those ads because the return was good. However, there came a time when this owner who had been buying those ads for years suddenly was not getting any calls on them. In fact, one week he did not get a single, solitary phone call! This was really unusual. Since he had built a relationship with the advertising company and had the historical data, he was able to show them his history of the number of leads that typically came and the lack of leads from this advertisement. Because of these factors, they were willing to work with him. They ended up giving him several weeks of advertising at no cost. I cannot say for sure, but I am pretty certain that if he did not have the long history of tracking, he would not have been able to negotiate to such a point.

> *B*ecause he had the historical data to back it up, when he didn't get the results he expected, he was able to negotiate better pricing.

There are advertising agencies out there that are willing to work with you. If you find the one who will take a little risk and be paid very fairly based on results, you have found a treasure. Most people will run! If they are a runner, do you really want to do business with them when they do not have confidence in their own marketing? You want to find the ones that will work with you and really care about your sales that come as a result of their marketing. Those are the ones who will put a little of their own skin in the game and put their money where their mouths – and promises – are.

There was another agency that sold space in a phone book. We all know how online has taken over a lot of phone publications, and this type of advertising has had to really recreate themselves. But still, for some people and some industries, it still pays to have an ad in a certain telephone book.

This certain business owner that I'll call Bob, explained that he was tired of paying $4,700 each month for less than ample returns. In order for this ad to work for him, he would need a certain number of guaranteed leads. After their song and dance, Bob asked if they would guarantee at least 100 leads per month or allow him to void his contract. The sales rep was agreeable, and made it part of the contract. Needless to say, after sending copies of his lead count, Bob ended up voiding his contract because he was unable to get the hundred leads that had been guaranteed.

Use your data to work for you when you are negotiating for different types of advertising!

In the sample chart above, it also includes lead cost. This is important, but not the end all or the determining factor as to whether or not to keep advertising with a certain lead source. It becomes more important once you start to look at the conversion of the leads. Right now, all you can really see is that some leads are more expensive to get than others. Since that is the case, it would make really good sense to assign those expensive leads to someone who will close them, and we will get into that more in-depth a little later.

Questions for Your Business:

1. Where do your leads come from?
2. What types of services are the leads from each service requesting?
3. How much does it cost to get a lead for each individual lead source?
4. What is the combined average cost for your company to get a lead?
5. On average, how long does it take for your company to convert from a lead to a sale?
6. How would it be helpful for you to know the cost of leads and how long the average sales cycle is?

NOTES

_____

_____

_____

_____

_____

_____

_____

_____

_____

_____

_____

_____

_____

_____

_____

Chapter 5

The Cost of Getting a Sale

Your company has a budget, and in order to make profits, that budget needs to be followed. A marketing budget could be blown in an instant when some of those marketers walk in the door and convince you that your business really will not survive unless you do a certain type of marketing. We've all been there. Unfortunately, if the marketing budget fluctuates outside the planned percentages, it usually means going over budget instead of under budget.

Fluctuating costs are not a bad thing if the increase in revenues is proportionate to the expense of marketing. It should not matter how much you spend, as long as you are able to keep your marketing and revenue percentages in balance with what was originally budgeted.

In order to get the most out of your marketing, you really do need to see what is working and what is not working. Then you are able to keep track of the bottom line, and if some forms of advertising take on a higher cost initially, the sales from low or no-cost advertising will need to step up to cover the difference. In order to do that however, there has to be a way to keep an eye on both the bottom line, as well as the individual advertising sources.

Just recently I had an interesting conversation with someone who was trying to sell me marketing. His whole premise was that in order to make sales, you need to do the marketing first. Yes, I agree with that. But then he said that marketing and sales are totally separate things. "You need me to do your marketing, and then you need someone to go out there and sell." This is where I totally disagree. Sales and marketing need to be talking to each other…all the time!

Your salespeople can give you very valuable feedback as to what they are hearing on the front lines. Make your marketing message be one that resonates with the people you are trying to attract. It does not matter how nice you think the message is; if your prospects are not moved to take action, then it is not a good message. Your salespeople, the ones on the front lines, would be the ones to get that valuable insight. Listen to them so that you can adjust your message to what your clients are wanting. Sometimes you can have the same exact product, and two entirely different messages. One message converts, while another does not. Again, it does not matter how beautiful your website is, how grand your brochures are, how snazzy the radio advertisement is, or how fantastic your videos are if they are not converting!

You can spend marketing money until you are blue in the face, but if it is not giving the return you need, it is not worth it. Whether the issue is with your sales team, in the marketing message itself, or in the demographics of people it is reaching, if it does not work, it does not pay to spend the money on it. Period.

There are ways that you can zero in on the issue to find out what the problem is, but unless you can find, see, and fix the problem in order to gain a return on a certain type of advertising, it does not pay to buy it.

On the same token, if you are spending money on marketing that is bringing in a nice return at a price that is working for your budget, then it pays to do it. And maybe it even pays to put more money there, depending on what the venue is and what is predicted to happen if you increase the spending to that source. But you still need to see what is giving you a return on your investment, and to what extent.

Let's take a quick look.

Here you have some of the most important numbers for getting real quick feedback on marketing effectiveness. This is not all inclusive, and there are other pieces that would be good to add to it, but in order to keep it real simple, I am laying it out like this.

Lead Source	Sales for Service 1	Sales for Service 2	Total Sales	Ad Costs	Ad % of Sales
Radio	$100,000	$30,000	$130,000	$7,000	5.3%
Direct Mail	$14,266	$20,000	$34,266	$800	2.3%
Trade Show	$25,734	$0	$25,734	$5,000	19.4%
Referrals	$90,000	$90,000	$195,000	$0	0%
Prev. Customers	$140,000	$80,000	$215,000	$0	0%
TOTAL	**$360,000**	**$240,000**	**$600,000**	**$12,800**	**2.1%**

The first number to look at is the percentage in the lower right corner. My company has budgeted 10% of gross sales for marketing, and since the company is at 2.1% overall, we are doing okay. In fact, we could probably stand to spend more. As I scan up the column, there is the 19.4% for the Trade Show that sticks out! This means that 19.4% of every contract I wrote for the Trade Show went to cover the cost of getting that sale. That means I spent almost two times more than I had budgeted to get that sale. So before even going any further on those sales, my business already lost a big percentage of profits from the Trade Show sales.

On the other hand, in the place where my company is spending the most money, the radio, my marketing is coming in at 5.3% of the overall sales. A few things are happening here, with the main point being my sales are high enough to justify the high cost of advertising. Since the allowance is for 10%, these sales are looking real nice, and, as long as the price point and cost of sales were made at the profitable margins, this advertising is working well for us.

Remember back to the Lead Count chart when it looked like we had a real dandy Trade Show because we had 92 leads? And the lead count for the radio station appeared to be low? Sometimes the actual number of leads is not so important; what really matters is what sells, at what volume, and at what cost to you.

Using this information, you can determine a few other things, too. For example, the 19.4% cost of getting a sale alerts you to investigate a bit. In this example, it only shows two sales so nobody's closing ratios are that great; however, if you had a fair number of leads and sales, then you could go to the individual salespeople to see if anyone is selling this lead source at a higher rate than others. If so, what is he or she doing differently than the others? Is it something that can be taught to the others? (We will get into more of this later.) There are other things to consider, too, such as when was the show? Have those leads had sufficient time to convert?

It might be worth it to mention here that I am in no way saying or even alluding to trade shows not working. This was just for the sake of showing how you measure. Trade shows have worked for us, and have worked well. Some work better than others, though. It can be a show put on by the same management, but at different times of the year or in different locations around the city. We track every show and have found patterns for where and when the buyers come. Now there are certain months and places we simply do not do shows because they do not work. On the other hand, we are eager to sign up even a year ahead of time for the ones that really work for us.

If you have no one who is able to close leads from certain advertising, it would make sense for you to quit that advertising. What would happen if you took that $5000 and put it toward advertising that worked for you? Would your sales increase proportionately to the amount of money you put in? Perhaps, perhaps not. But the chances are they would increase somewhat anyhow. And if you do not want to put that money toward other advertising, at least cut the advertising that does not work, and save yourself the money for something else.

There is a great example of this from one man's roofing business. He was at $2.5 million in gross revenues, and his advertising costs were $272,000. His overall cost of getting a sale was very close to, but a little over, his budgeted 10%. He was not doing too bad overall; however, when he glanced up and down the column he saw several advertising venues that clearly were not working, and some that really were. Within 13 months, he reallocated some of those marketing dollars to places that were working, and totally cut $100,000 for advertising was flat out not working. At the same time sales increased by $400,000 through advertising that was working. The cost of sale acquisition also came down to 5.8%. That made for a net difference of half a million dollars in 13 months. For a small business, that is money worth talking about!

Another way you can use a brief chart like this, especially when you are offering different services, is to see what advertising is bringing in the leads and sales for each type of service. Sometimes it is very good to split test (super easy to do on websites or with email blasts) to see what message is hitting home with your prospects. What is it that makes them pick up the phone to call you or email you? If you are advertising in a zip code with million dollar homes, they probably are not interested in the value pack advertisement for Formica countertops or cheap carpet cleaning. They are going to be picky about who they let into their homes. Instead, they might pay more attention to the trucks in the neighbor's driveway, the local magazines they get from their neighborhood associations, or the person they hear about while at the local spa or gym. The options are endless, but the point is, pay attention who is getting the advertising you are sending out.

One of the companies I helped with marketing advertised for many years with a couple different radio stations. When the housing market started to decline, their leads from one of the stations dramatically dipped, and the sales became harder and harder to make. The sales that did come in were at a very low average contract size. It was strange because that particular radio station had historically been a great source of sales for them from the very beginning when they opened their doors, but now it was like pulling hen's teeth to get a sale.

The radio station was on top of what was going on. They knew the lack of leads, and there was frequent communication back and forth, and adjustments were made to the message. After some time of seeing no return on investment, it was time for the company to consider pulling their radio ads. Before quitting, though, the radio station jumped over backwards to try to make it work. Besides changing up the message, changing the services offered (this company offered several), changing the frequency and times, this station really brainstormed and put out surveys to their listening audience. What they found out was a repeat of what the company records said; the people did not have ready cash. It was a time when banks were no longer lending, and the people who listened to this particular station were a younger generation. The listeners of the other station were an older generation, they had ready cash, and did not need to depend on the bank to make their buying decisions. It paid for them to be able to focus on the people with cash.

After spending many years with certain radio personalities and having great success, the company had developed a good relationship and almost a loyalty to the station. This was not an easy decision, but when it was driven by the numbers, there was not one of the eight people present in that meeting room that could not say it was the right decision.

> *I*t was not an easy decision, but when driven by the numbers, they all knew it was right.

There are times when a certain advertising source may cost a bit more. For example, if you are just starting radio advertising, it takes a while to get noticed. Depending on the type of advertising you do, there may be a lag time, so be sure to find out what you should expect, and then plan for that. If they say it is going to take six months before you start to see a return, then plan on that.

That initial lag time is okay, as long as you plan for it in the overall scheme of marketing. If the cost of one lead source is higher, then the cost of other lead sources needs to be lower in order to compensate and balance out your company total. Give and take, give and take; it's a continuous balancing act.

By giving and taking in the balancing act, you have to continuously keep an eye on the bottom line. If you are going to spend money on more expensive venues or venues with a lag in the return, you and your people must offset that by selling low or no-cost marketing: self-generated, referrals, and previous customers. By getting sales there, you are able to offset the higher cost advertising until it starts to pay for itself.

Another thing to consider is that once you start making some sales from the higher-cost advertising, it is good to have your referral program in place so that you and your salespeople can reap the benefits of secondary sales through either referrals or repeat customers. Ideally, we pay a higher cost initially to get low or no cost down the road.

Some advertising can be very expensive, but if you are getting a return on it proportionate to what you have budgeted, then it is working for you, and the actual dollar amount does not matter. As long as you see the return, continue advertising with them. And smile as you hand over the checks.

It is just a part of doing business. Spend wisely now, and reap the benefits for the lifetime of a customer. When you are going to take on some higher cost advertising, make sure to plan for the long haul because some of it takes an investment of time and money. But at the same time, make sure to compensate for the higher cost in those areas by bringing in enough sales through low cost or no cost advertising in order to keep your overall marketing in line with what was budgeted.

Questions for Your Business:

1. What percent of your budget is allotted for marketing?
2. During the past 12 months, what percentage of gross revenues has been spent on marketing?
3. If the answer to Question 2 is higher than Question 1, you have lost from what was to have been part of Profits. Why is there a discrepancy?
4. What is your overall Cost of Getting a Sale in dollars and percentage? (Total Marketing Cost divided by Total Gross Revenues)
5. What advertising brings in the highest revenues?
6. What advertising brings in the best ROI or Acquisition Cost? (When looking at your percentage of advertising costs

compared to revenues generated, which has the lowest percentage?) This is marketing that is working for you. How can you duplicate it?

7. What advertising has the lowest ROI (When looking at your percentage of advertising costs compared to revenues generated, which has the *highest* percentage)? How could you bring this number down?

8. What type of system do you use to follow the return on your individual advertising campaigns as well as overall marketing so that you can adjust it as needed?

NOTES

_____

_____

_____

_____

_____

_____

_____

_____

_____

_____

_____

_____

_____

_____

Chapter 6

Salesperson Effectiveness

One of the most common Google searches people use in coming to my website is, 'What is a good closing ratio?' Closing ratios play an important part in evaluating salespeople, but it is certainly not the most important. In fact, it is a secondary number that you examine! But, in answer to that question, there are standards that can define the typical closing ratio by industry, though your company may have different expectations within it.

Before you look at individual closing ratios you should know: What does it cost for each of your salespeople to make a sale? Where are they in comparison to what your budget allows? You should know this by individual lead source or advertising source, as well as total advertising sources.

If those costs are in line with what is required in order for you to run profitably, then you can go to examine the closing ratios and sales volume to see how they are doing there. If you had very high dollar volume sales from a rep that had a low closing ratio, you would not necessarily say that person is not good for you, even though their closing ratio is low. However, it would only make sense for you to see what can be done to help that person close at a higher rate.

On the other hand, if you see over a period of time that it continues to cost you more than you have budgeted for a salesperson to make a sale, you are going backwards, because the overage cost is coming directly from your profits, at least for that specific form of advertising. If you balance the volume of sales from high cost advertising with more sales from low cost or no cost advertising so the total sales and cost percentages are in line with your overall budget, you are okay in the long run. But at the same time you want to focus on the individual advertising, too, because it only makes sense to try to get the most you can out of each individual advertising venue. You must have a way to see if the costs of getting sales are coming in on target with your budget, or not.

Once you know what it is costing to get sales from specific advertising venues, then you can start to look at the volume and closing ratio. If you have one person who is selling jobs profitably, but has a low closing ratio, what can you do to help them close higher? Is more training necessary? Do they need more product information? Do they need to learn more about upselling? Do they need to be bolder in offering higher ticket items?

A certain business owner had a pretty nice-sized company with around fifteen sales representatives at any given time. He figured some of those people were profitable, but was not quite sure *how* profitable. There were others that gave him the gut feeling that even though their closing ratios were nice, it just did not seem that they were making the company money because the money in the till was not substantial. Have you ever had that feeling?

They were also spending a lot of money (around $400,000 each year) on different kinds of advertising, and some of that advertising was more expensive than others. The thought in the back of their minds was that they wanted to be able to assign those expensive leads to the people who could sell them. By getting the best bang for their buck, he knew that it would be a win-win-win all the way around.

If they could figure out a way to determine who was good at selling what kinds of leads, they would be able to assign those leads to that person(s). Even more importantly, if they knew someone was *not* good at selling certain leads, they would *not* want to give him those leads. By putting everyone in places where they are strong, the customer wins because they are getting what they originally called about, the sales reps win because their close rates and sales volume increase, and the company wins because revenues go up, (given of course that the pricing structure was good, too).

Taking those thoughts, his company hired a woman who worked doggedly day in and day out to track every single lead that came into the office. Mind you, this was not so many years ago, but before they had lead, sales, and marketing tracking software that had been developed especially for small businesses, so all this work was by paper and pencil. Believe me, with technology nowadays, there's a better, faster and easier way now.

Each month before the monthly sales meeting, she would spend up to *three nights at the office* compiling the data, and getting it laid out the best she could. Over time they were able to keep a pretty good eye on the sales and marketing numbers of their business. They began to have data that was strong enough for them to make reliable sales decisions which were dependent on marketing results and marketing decisions that were made dependent upon sales. Sales and marketing were totally interwoven.

> They began to have data they could use to make reliable sales decisions.

In the graphs below, some basic types of data she needed are outlined. This is focusing on totals only, and not divided into product or service, which is also very helpful and important to have. But walk through it with me to catch the gist of what I want to explain, and you will begin to see how basic data can be collected and manipulated in a number of ways to get information that will help you in the same way it helped this business owner mentioned above.

We have Johnny and Suzy, sales representatives of the same company. They both have had similar lengths of experience with the company, and both have approximately the same number of leads from each advertising source, with the exception of Referrals and Previous Customers.

Johnny Salesrep

Lead Source	# of Leads	# of Sales	Closing %	Total Sales	Ad Costs	Ad % of Sales
Radio	8	3	38%	100,000	$3,500	3.5%
Direct Mail	5	1	20%	5,200	$364	7%
Trade Show	46	8	17%	5,000	$2,500	44%
Referrals	8	7	88%	15,000	$0	0%
Prev. Customers	31	19	61%	180,000	$0	0%
TOTAL	98	38	39%	$305,200	$6,364	2.0%

Suzy Salesrep

Lead Source	# of Leads	# of Sales	Closing %	Total Sales	Ad Costs	Ad % of Sales
Radio	8	1	13%	30,000	$3,500	44%
Direct Mail	6	3	50%	29,066	$436	1.5%
Trade Show	46	4	9%	20,734	$2,500	3%
Referrals	16	8	50%	180,000	$0	0%
Prev. Customers	7	2	29%	35,000	$0	0%
TOTAL	83	18	22%	$294,800	$6,436	2.1%

At first glance, you see that Johnny has a much higher closing ratio than Suzy, but when you look to the Total Sales, they are rather close. When you look all the way to the right, you will see the 2.0% and 2.1% for the Total Ad % of Sales.

That means overall, it costs the company approximately 2% off the top of each of their sales to cover the cost of advertising, the cost of bringing in the sale. If the marketing budget allows for 10%, then they are both doing fantastic from that perspective. *This is the percentage that a business owner or manager should look at first when checking out a salesperson's effectiveness.* From there, the effectiveness can be worked backwards to examine other numbers, including closing ratios or percentages.

Even though Suzy has a much lower-than-desired closing ratio, we are not going to show her the door yet, because she is bringing in sales at a very low cost to us. Our challenge now is to see what we can do to help her increase her overall closing ratio. You see, several things are going through my mind while I'm looking at this: 1. Suzy is bringing in a fair amount of revenues, 2. Her cost of getting a sale is great, 3. Her closing ratio is terrible, so that means there are a lot leads she is not closing, a lot of wasted leads somewhere, a lot of money left on the table.

How can I, as her manager or the business owner, look at where she is strong and let her sell there? If she was allowed to sell in places where she is strong, her overall closing ratio would increase, along with her revenues. Or how can I, as her manager or the business owner, find out what the others are doing to close in the areas she is not closing, and transfer that knowledge or knack to her? How can I train her? Or is it something that can be learned? If it is not something that is easily transferable, would it make sense to assign those leads to someone who will close them?

Let's look closer.

Even though both of these representatives are performing well overall, you can pick out some alerts. Keeping in mind the marketing budget, skim up and down the right column where it says Ad % of Sale.

Johnny Salesrep

Lead Source	# of Leads	# of Sales	Closing %	Total Sales	Ad Costs	Ad % of Sales
Radio	8	3	38%	120,000	$3,500	2.9%
Direct Mail	5	1	20%	5,200	$364	7%
Trade Show	46	8	17%	5,000	$2,500	44%
Referrals	8	7	88%	15,000	$0	0%
Prev. Customers	31	19	61%	180,000	$0	0%
TOTAL	**98**	**38**	**39%**	**$325,200**	**$6,364**	**2.0%**

Suzy Salesrep

Lead Source	# of Leads	# of Sales	Closing %	Total Sales	Ad Costs	Ad % of Sales
Radio	8	1	13%	10,000	$3,500	35%
Direct Mail	6	3	50%	29,066	$436	1.5%
Trade Show	46	4	9%	20,734	$2,500	3%
Referrals	16	8	50%	180,000	$0	0%
Prev. Customers	7	2	29%	35,000	$0	0%
TOTAL	**83**	**18**	**22%**	**$274,800**	**$6,436**	**2.3%**

In looking at Johnny, you can see that even though his overall closing ratio is very nice, he has certain lead sources where he is not strong. Direct mail and trade shows, in this case. Why is he not closing those? Well, maybe because those are pretty cold leads, even colder than the radio where the host has spoken so fondly of your company. Whatever the reason, he is obviously not doing well with them, so if you cannot train him in ways to sell them, then do not give those leads to him. Give them to someone who will sell them. By doing so, you will not only allow him to use his time to close where he is strong, but you will allow the next person to close where they are strong, too. If no one in your company can sell them, then either hire someone who can or quit advertising there.

Suzy is not making your company any money through her radio sales. Since the marketing budget for this company allows for 10%, in order for it to be profitable to give Suzy leads from the radio from a marketing standpoint, she needs to bring in sales ten times the cost of what the company is spending. Her sales should be $35,000 at a minimum. Right now it is costing the company 35% off the top of each of her sales just to make the sale. That is nearly 3 ½ times what was budgeted, your profits were eaten, and in fact, your company went backwards on her radio sales.

Johnny, on the other hand, is doing well for us with the radio leads. He brought in $120,000 in comparison to Suzy's $10,000, and his average contract was $40,000, while her only sale was $10,000. The cost of Johnny bringing in a sale is decent, the sales revenues are good, and his closing ratio is acceptable.

Now put the data of the two of them together to examine the total company averages.

The company ended up paying 5.3% on average to cover the cost of advertising for each radio sale. That is good, because they budgeted for 10% or less.

Company Totals

Lead Source	# of Leads	# of Sales	Closing %	Total Sales	Ad Costs	Ad % of Sales
Radio	16	4	21%	130,000	$7,000	5.3%
Direct Mail	11	4	50%	34,266	$800	2.3%
Trade Show	92	12	7%	25,734	$5,000	19%
Referrals	24	15	50%	195,000	$0	0%
Prev. Customers	38	21	29%	215,000	$0	0%
TOTAL	181	56	31%	$600,000	$12,800	2.1%

However, there is some obvious waste here, so what can be done? What is Johnny doing that Suzy is not doing? Is it something that can be helped through training? Could she learn it? Does she need more product knowledge? Not only does she need to increase her closing ratio, but it looks indeed like she is leaving money on the table since Johnny is able to bring in much higher contracts.

Imagine if all those leads had been assigned to Johnny. This is just an example to keep it simple, but still, the concept is there. Suppose Johnny was given all 16 leads, and closed 38% of them for a grand total of 6 sales. Multiply that by his average contract of $40,000 and you have $240,000. The company could have possibly had sales of $240,000 instead of $130,000 by assigning this to their best closer. Would that make a difference for you in your company when something like this is repeated several times over?

Not only would the company have benefitted in sales volume, but Johnny and his customers would have, also. His customers would have been able to buy, his commissions would have increased, and at the same time Suzy would have had greater success in an area where she was good. That is how you get a win-win-win all the way around.

When you start to tie the marketing to sales, you most definitely will start to see trends among your sales representatives and the advertising they sell best. There are reasons for that. Each person is an individual, their customers are individuals, and some people click better than others with certain demographics.

Consider your advertising. What are the demographics of people that are receiving that advertising? Conservative, liberal, young, old, affluent, middle-class, lower-income, free-spirited, concrete-sequential personalities? Who are they? You need to know.

If you take the radio, for example, there are certain demographics that listen to each station. For starters, it would only make sense for you to know a radio station's listening audience before you start advertising. Make sure that your product or service is something that sells to those demographics, and then when those people call your office, set them up with one of the representatives who can sell best to that personality of people, maybe even one who listens to the same station.

Here is a real example from another company with whom I am associated. They have spent hundreds of thousands of dollars on radio advertising with several stations over the past 10 years. There is one particular station that has brought in some rather qualified buyers who hold cash. The listening audience has a lot of older conservatives. Well, there is a hard-core conservative in the office, and when he gets a lead like that, in his mind it is sold before he even meets the prospect.

Meanwhile, there is another person who is a rather seasoned salesperson, knows the product and service inside out, and does well with certain types of prospects, but certainly not this particular listening audience.

This company was to a point where they needed to seriously consider cutting the advertising on that radio station because the year-to-date sales acquisition cost was 39% for all of the sales team combined for that station. With a budget allowing 10%, they were paying about four times what they had budgeted percentage-wise, and it was clearly not working for the company!

At the same time, they were distributing leads in a round robin way. They just went down the line and gave the next lead to the next in line.

There was an announcement to the sales team that advertising on the station may be cut because the low sales volume from that station did not justify the cost of advertising. There was almost mutiny in that sales room, as the one representative in particular felt that station was his bread and butter, and he had the best success with them. (Ahem, mind you, his overall cost of getting a sale was 31% at the time.)

There was some time before that company would need to renew their contract with the radio station, so they had time to work with the reps. After some discussion, it was decided that going forward, the lead distribution would be based on who was selling what. In other words, radio sales and any other type of paid advertising would be distributed based on a predetermined performance. As long as a person was selling what was expected of them for any lead source, they would continue to get leads from that source. If not, further leads would not be given to them until they went back and closed some of the prior leads and brought their cost percentages down.

The company gave a couple months for them to work their existing leads, and agreed that as long as it was profitable, the radio advertising would continue. Otherwise the contract was not going to be renewed. By the end of two months, the top radio salesperson was at 13% cost of getting a sale, and heading in the right direction toward 10%. The highest costing radio salesperson was at 51%. The leads continued to be distributed for the lowest cost sales rep, and ended for the highest cost sales rep.

Today, the sales representative whose cost of getting a sale was 31% is now at a 7.56%, and the company overall is at 8.1%. His closing ratio for that radio station went from 27% to 47%, and his average contract from that station went from $14,000 to $39,000.

The high cost sales rep did not crumble under the pressure of having to increase his revenues in order to get more leads; instead, the company expectations motivated him to really work his existing leads, and brought his cost down from 51% to approximately 3%, and he is now the front runner for getting those radio leads!

In addition to that, the company recently took a look at their overall sales from that radio station. In comparing their billable sales from January through August 2013 to billable sales in January through August 2014, there was an increase of a little over $1 million from that radio station.

Their salespeople were made aware of the expectations and rose to the occasion. This was the mark of some very talented and determined salespeople, salespeople you want on your team. They became determined once they understood the company had very specific expectations of their sales performance.

> *The salespeople became determined once they understood the company had specific expectations of their performance.*

Remember that I said in his mind the sale was made already before the salespeople met the customer? I asked him about it. He said, "Oh, I know that as soon as I get a lead from that radio station, I'm going into that home on a totally different level than any other salesperson." He went on to explain that he goes there knowing that they already have some things in common, they think alike, and the relationship is easier to build. Any one of us in sales knows that most sales are made in the mind of the salesperson ahead of time. That is a truth. So if a salesperson is so keen on selling certain types of leads, why not assign them that way?

The sales rep who was not initially selling to that listening audience had found a comfortable niche among previous customers and referrals. He still sells those like crazy, and would way rather have those warm leads instead of any other leads anyhow. While that particular company will spend money to acquire new business, this type of sale is actually preferable because the referrals are a great way to continue building the customer base, and at a very low-cost to the company.

One more important piece of measuring the effectiveness of a salesperson is looking at the actual cost of sale (COS) at which they brought in a contract. By cost of sale, I mean the hard costs, the labor and material to deliver the product or service you deliver. This is a line that should stand out on its own. In order to be profitable for the company, your price lists should reflect that, and the salesperson should be pricing the sale profitably.

There are times when a salesperson may have some room to budge a bit, but it does not pay to keep writing sales at a higher cost than would be profitable for you to deliver. There are checks and balances in several places. Let's say that a rep was writing a sale for a self-generated lead. That marketing did not cost much, if anything. He might have a little wiggle room, as long as the whole picture does not go out of focus. On the other hand, when you start tracking the cost of sale tied to both the salesperson and the advertising venue, you may see that some reps bring in a sufficient number of sales, but they are all at a high cost of sale, or the average is at a high cost of sale.

This can mean one of a few different things: 1) The sales rep is lowering the price just to get the sale, 2) the audience or demographics of that advertising source will not pay the prices you need or are asking, 3) your price lists needs updating.

In the case of the representative lowering the price, there has to be a limit. If he/she wants to give up some commissions to cover the difference in order to get a sale, that is okay at times. There are times, depending on the type, that a sale can be made at a little higher cost of sale. However, in the case of a sales rep continuously bringing in high cost of sales contracts, it is probably an issue with the competence of the rep. Is it a lack of boldness in asking for the sale at a profitable price? Maybe your rep himself is not a total believer in what he is selling, or has not been clear enough in creating a real value for the customer. Who knows? There can be many reasons. However, you will go backwards if you make too many sales at a cost higher than you have budgeted. That sales rep will need to either have some training or otherwise be shown the door, because in order for you to make money, sales need to be made while keeping your profit margins in mind. Besides that, sales reps should make their full commissions. It's good to keep them with that thought at the top of their minds; it's not a good practice for them to always take a cut.

Some of us have seen the salesperson who has gone out and written a lot of sales…at a price way too low. It becomes a norm for the weak salesperson. It is not nice to be on the business operations side of things, looking over the contract and seeing that the price list was not followed. Often, we have to either send that salesperson back to ask for more money or cancel the job. Even worse is if we have completed that job and find them coming in at a high cost of sale, one after another.

As for the demographics of an advertising source not paying your prices, you are not going to get Mercedes prices in a Chevy Spark neighborhood. There will be times that the demographics will pay your prices, and there will be times that the demographics will not pay your prices. If the only way your salespeople can get sales from certain advertising is to lower the prices, then quit advertising there. If you have some salespeople that can make nice, profitable sales from the same neighborhoods and there are sales to be had, send them there. If no one is selling there, it probably makes sense to cancel the advertising. However, if even one of your sales reps is successfully selling from that advertising to those demographics, they have proven sales can be made, and you will need to adjust your training or your lead assignment in order to make your advertising in that venue profitable for you.

The third possibility is that your price lists needing adjusting. If all your sales are coming in at a high cost of sale, there is a real possibility that your pricing is too low. We've had some crazy years recently, and the fluctuation of oil prices kept painting and roofing business owners on their toes, among many others. The prices of supplies were constantly changing according to the price of oil, and in order to keep running profitably, the price schedules had to change right alongside the oil in order to transfer the cost of supplies to the consumer.

These are just some of the numbers that you want to be able to keep a constant eye on in determining the proper pricing and salesperson effectiveness. When you have a way to do that, then everything else becomes a whole lot easier and more productive.

When you bring in new sales representatives, show them how you measure their success, and that you run your business by the numbers. In the beginning, allow them a certain dollar amount or number of leads to get them going, and give them a chance to start writing some sales. At the same time, in order to offset the high cost of getting a sale for them initially, it would be in their best interests to start soliciting leads on their own, too. If they do not offset the cost, it will be up to you or the rest of the company to offset it or carry the load in order to not slide backwards as a whole.

> *When* you bring in new sales reps, show them how you measure their success.

I am a former elementary school teacher. I have seen across the ages that no matter how old we are, most people tend to perform best when they know what is expected of them, whether those measureable expectations and goals have been set by them or someone else. High expectations equal high results; low or no expectations equal low or no results. If you have a system in place, and allow your sales people easy access to see their numbers and where they stand, the motivated one will perform to expectations, just like the hard-core conservative who was afraid of losing his radio station. The one who is not motivated probably will not appreciate the numbers so, if that is the case, you do not want that person on your team anyhow.

That is part of the beauty of having systems in place, too. You do not need to get in sticky, emotional situations with anyone when everyone is on the same page. Everyone understands what is expected of them, how they are measured, and they are given the tools to make it happen. You do not have to find yourself trying to defend lead assignment, people are not grouching about getting all the rotten leads, and your salespeople can see that they are treated fairly. As long as they are performing to expectations, all is well. Their success means your success. As a business owner, there is nothing more beautiful than being able to provide the tools for your people to perform to your expectations, and at the level in which you are able to make profits.

Questions for Your Business:

1. When you consider the individuals on your sales team, how do you determine what it costs (the sales acquisition costs) for each one to bring in a sale?
2. If you do not know what it costs for them to bring in a sale, how do you determine whether or not they are profitable?
3. Do you know which products or services each of your salespeople sell most profitably for your business?
4. Do you know which lead sources each of your salespeople sell most profitably?
5. Do you know your sales reps closing ratios for paid and unpaid advertising? Are those in sync with industry standards and your expectations?
6. How could you use data from individual closing ratios to help your sales team?
7. What could happen in your business if you had a way to assign leads to each salesperson's strengths?
8. Are you certain your salesperson with the highest closing ratio is really your *best* salesperson from a *profit* standpoint?

NOTES

_____

_____

_____

_____

_____

_____

_____

_____

_____

_____

_____

_____

_____

_____

Chapter 7

A Common Misunderstanding in Measuring ROI

Can You Spot the Mistake?

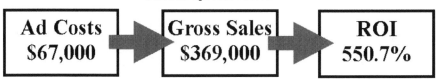

| Ad Costs $67,000 | Gross Sales $369,000 | ROI 550.7% |

Just this past week, a company with whom I work on their advertising was talking to different radio stations to find a good fit of station and radio show personality for their company. The radio station submitted a packet to the company that included a case study to prove the success of a certain Show Host's endorsements as follows:

Case Study #1
Radio Station: Show Host Listeners Spend Money!
(In order to protect privacy, the name of the national show host, radio station, and company has been changed to Show Host, Radio Station, and ABC Company.)

"Show Host has been endorsing ABC Company for several years. ABC Company knows when Show Host endorses a product or service, his audience is listening – and Show Host has numbers to prove it. In 2010, Show Host's endorsement, a $67,000 investment, brought ABC Company $369,000. That's a 550.7% return on investment!"

Do you recognize the fallacy here? In this case as illustrated above, there was a positive return on investment, but certainly nowhere near 550.7%! Unfortunately, this is a very common misconception among people buying advertising.

For someone who is not tuned into the numbers, this is a very common misunderstanding, and a can be a costly price to pay for not knowing what to expect from your marketing efforts. Any company that advertises should know the results they need to reach for expected profitability. Know your budget and your margins.

To make it real simple, if ABC Company has a marketing budget of 10%, that means if they spent $67,000 on advertising with this show host, they should have gotten around $670,000 in gross sales before this advertising would have given the profits they planned for. If their advertising budget was around 5%, which is probably more common for many companies, gross sales should have been $1,340,000.

In figuring out a real ROI, the actual cost of delivering the product or service, overhead, and commissions all have to be included *in addition to* the cost of advertising in order to figure out profits, which then become the dollar amount for measuring the Return on Investment percentage.

The headline of the advertisement from this radio station that was proudly showing a huge return on investment was totally misleading, even though I really believe they did not intend it to be. Many marketers do not even realize that comparing only the dollars spent on advertising to the dollars taken in is incorrect and misleading. It will not lead to the full potential of your marketing dollars!

Based on a typical trades company, here is a pie graph to show where all the dollars would go in figuring out the true ROI on sales of $369,000 with $67,000 spent in marketing. In reality, a lot of service-related companies are selling at a 60% Cost of Sale or more, and some of the other percentages may fluctuate from company to company, but in this example we will say the sales were priced and sold at a 55% cost of sale.

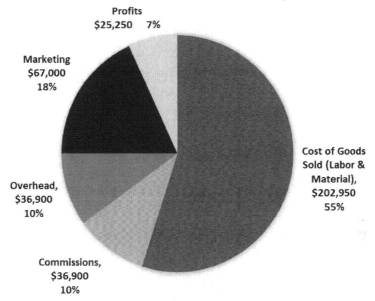

DISTRIBUTION OF SALES OF $369,000

Profits
$25,250   7%

Marketing
$67,000
18%

Cost of Goods
Sold (Labor &
Material),
$202,950
55%

Overhead,
$36,900
10%

Commissions,
$36,900
10%

Based on sales of $369,000, if:

- Cost of Sale (Typically labor and material) is priced at 55% or $202,950
- Commissions are 10% or $36,900
- Overhead is 10% or $36,900
- Marketing is 18% or $67,000

Then:

- Profits are 7% or $25,250

Your ROI is actually the comparison between Profits and what was spent, so in order to figure out the true ROI percentage, take your profit dollar amount and divide it by dollars spent on advertising. (Take the profit dollar amount of $25,250 and divide it by the marketing cost of $67,000 and you will end up with 37.7%, a true percentage for the Return on your Investment.)

Ad Costs $67,000	Gross Sales $369,000	Profits $25,250	ROI 37.7%

As you can see, even though there was a profitable ROI in the scenario above, there is a huge difference between the actual 37.7% and the 550.7% that the radio station had claimed to be the ROI.

I did get back in touch with the radio station after I had written an article about this on my blog, and they thanked me for not sharing their name. I believe it really, truly was a mistake on their part simply because, like many others, they did not know.

As a business owner, you need to know your numbers.

Questions for Your Business:

1. Would you have been able to recognize the error in the claim to a 550.7% ROI?
2. When you buy advertising, what are your revenue expectations for a return?
3. How do you measure to see that you are getting your expected and required Return on Investment in Marketing?

NOTES

_____

_____

_____

_____

_____

_____

_____

_____

_____

_____

_____

_____

_____

_____

_____

Chapter 8

Now That You Have the Numbers, How Can They Be Used for Planning?

Say it is the end of the year and it is time to look at next year. This can actually also be done any time you start any new marketing campaign or bring on new sales people, and does not have to be contained to the start of the year.

What do you want to do with your sales and marketing? Are you going to continue as you have been going, or are you going to initiate some changes?

You have been gathering sales and marketing data for a period of time, maybe a year or maybe even two or three, so now you have the information at your fingertips and the ability to use this information to help you plan for your company's goals and marketing efforts!

This is really not that difficult, but it will take some concentration. In fact, you are in a really good position to be able to start doing some goal-based marketing because your results are somewhat predictable, and your "Marketing-for-Sales-Results" can be much more intentional. In other words, your step-by-step system can predict a rather reliable ROI before you even start new advertising efforts, and you know what to expect from the very beginning. From the standpoint of a business owner, this is a great place to be. A person who is able to use history to plan for the future has a very solid framework from which to develop the rest. Without that, it's all a guessing game.

If you have been tracking leads, sales and marketing as described in the previous chapters, you will now have the numbers to help you know:

1. The average closing ratios on paid advertising and unpaid advertising for each sales rep individually and as a company.
2. The average dollar value of a sale.
3. How much you will need to spend to get enough leads for your salespeople to reach a certain amount in revenues.
4. How many leads you will need to allow your salespeople to close at their average rate to reach their sales goals at the ROI your company needs.
5. What your investment for marketing will need to be in the coming year or given time period in order to attain the revenues you are pursuing.

How do you use this information to determine the amount of money you want to spend, and the number of leads you need in order to achieve your company goals?

The best way to illustrate how to use your numbers is to show you some real numbers from a real company. I worked with them in planning their sales goals and marketing budget for the coming year.

Overall, their company did quite well the previous year, but they wanted to do better and start some planned growth.

What I did was go through their data, separate their salespeople's leads by paid and unpaid advertising, found out the closing ratio and average job revenues for paid and unpaid, and total revenues generated for both paid and unpaid advertising.

Here is the type of information to pull for each sales person, and the following graphs will show what kind of attention I give to each piece of information as I plan my sales and marketing goals.

Graph 1

Sales Rep 1	# of Leads	# of Closes	Revenue	Closing %	Ad Cost	Ad Cost % of Sales	Avg. Contract	Avg. Cost/Sale
Paid	81	17	$466,346.80	21.0%	$47,884.99	10.27%	$27,432.16	$2,816.76
Unpaid	47	17	$672,808.30	36.2%	$0.00	0.00%	$39,576.96	$0.00
Totals	128	34	$1,139,155.10	26.6%	$47,884.99	4.20%	$33,504.56	$1,408.38

Graph 1 shows the numbers for each sales rep, as well as the company's numbers as a whole. You can see that Sales Rep 1 had 128 leads during the year, 81 of which were from Paid Advertising, and 47 of which were from Unpaid Advertising (referrals, previous customers and self-generated).

His 21.0% closing ratio for Paid Advertising was considerably lower than the closing ratio of 36.2% for Unpaid Advertising, which makes total sense. Referrals and previous customers already have prior buying experience with you and should naturally close at a higher rate.

Graph 2

Sales Rep 1	# of Leads	# of Closes	Revenue	Closing %	Ad Cost	Ad Cost % of Sales	Avg. Contract	Avg. Cost/Sale
Paid	81	17	$466,346.80	21.0%	$47,884.99	10.27%	$27,432.16	$2,816.76
Unpaid	47	17	$672,808.30	36.2%	$0.00	0.00%	$39,576.96	$0.00
Totals	128	34	$1,139,155.10	26.6%	$47,884.99	4.20%	$33,504.56	$1,408.38

In Graph 2 above, notice the difference in the Average Contract amounts between Paid and Unpaid Advertising. The Average Contract for Paid Advertising sales is $27,432.16, whereas the Average Contract for Unpaid Advertising sales is $39,576.96.

The Paid Advertising is necessary to bring in new customers to some extent, and they will eventually become previous and return customers, but when you look at the numbers on this, a salesperson will see that it makes so much more sense to spend time cultivating those relationships with their previous customers.

Graph 3

Now looking at Graph 3 below, you can see that the average cost of getting a sale through Paid Advertising $2,816.76, and the average contract size is $27,432.16. The cost of getting leads from Unpaid Advertising is just as its name insinuates, unpaid or very low if you pay referral fees or self-generated bonuses of some sort. The cost is next to nothing, and the average contract is much more than the average Paid Advertising contract.

Sales Rep 1	# of Leads	# of Closes	Revenue	Closing %	Ad Cost	Ad Cost % of Sales	Avg. Contract	Avg. Cost/Sale
Paid	81	17	$466,346.80	21.0%	$47,884.99	10.27%	$27,432.16	$2,816.76
Unpaid	47	17	$672,808.30	36.2%	$0.00	0.00%	$39,576.96	$0.00
Totals	128	34	$1,139,155.10	26.6%	$47,884.99	4.20%	$33,504.56	$1,408.38

With very minimal costs of Unpaid advertising, and sales that generate much higher revenues with Unpaid Advertising, it is a WIN all the way around. It only makes sense that the company would want to do more to promote and generate more leads among the current customer database, whether it is actual repeat sales to previous customers or referrals from those who have benefitted from your products or services.

Now let's look at Sales Rep 2.

Graph 4

Sales Rep 2	# of Leads	# of Closes	Revenue	Closing %	Ad Cost	Ad Cost % of Sales	Avg. Contract	Avg. Cost/Sale
Paid	90	23	$765,233.00	25.6%	$67,270.00	8.79%	$33,271.00	$2,924.78
Unpaid	30	19	$116,102.00	63.3%	$0.00	0.00%	$6,110.63	$0.00
Totals	120	42	$881,335.00	35.0%	$67,270.00	7.63%	$20,984.17	$1,601.67

In Graph 4 above, you can see that Sales Rep 2 had 120 leads during the year, 90 of which were from Paid Advertising, and 30 of which were from Unpaid Advertising (referrals, previous customers and self-generated).

His closing ratio for Paid Advertising was 25.6%, which is 4.6 percentage points higher than the closing ratio of 21.0% that Sales Rep 1 had for Paid Advertising.

The closing ratio for Unpaid Advertising was 63.3%. Looks good, but is it really?

Graph 5

Sales Rep 2	# of Leads	# of Closes	Revenue	Closing %	Ad Cost	Ad Cost % of Sales	Avg. Contract	Avg. Cost/Sale
Paid	90	23	$765,233.00	25.6%	$67,270.00	8.79%	$33,271.00	$2,924.78
Unpaid	30	19	$116,102.00	63.3%	$0.00	0.00%	$6,110.63	$0.00
Totals	120	42	$881,335.00	35.0%	$67,270.00	7.63%	$20,984.17	$1,601.67

In looking at Graph 5, you see that the Average Contract for Paid Advertising for Sales Rep 2 is $33,271, or about $5800 higher per contract than Sales Rep 1. Another interesting thing you can see in Graph 4 is that, although Sales Rep 2 had a 63.3% Closing Ratio for Unpaid Advertising, the Average Contract was very low, only $6,110.63. That makes me ask the question, "What's going on here?" This needs to be addressed when working with the sales reps, but now for planning purposes, the numbers are the numbers.

Graph 6

Sales Rep 2	# of Leads	# of Closes	Revenue	Closing %	Ad Cost	Ad Cost % of Sales	Avg. Contract	Avg. Cost/Sale
Paid	90	23	$765,233.00	25.6%	$67,270.00	8.79%	$33,271.00	$2,924.78
Unpaid	30	19	$116,102.00	63.3%	$0.00	0.00%	$6,110.63	$0.00
Totals	120	42	$881,335.00	35.0%	$67,270.00	7.63%	$20,984.17	$1,601.67

In looking at Graph 6, most of the revenues for Sales Person 2 are coming from Paid Advertising. He is closing at 25.6% compared to Sales Person 1 at 21.0%, and the Average Contract size is higher, so he is a stronger closer of newer, colder leads than Sales Person 1.

However, results from Unpaid Advertising compared to Sales Person 1 are abysmal in two ways: first, there are many fewer Unpaid (referrals, previous customers and self-generated) leads than there are for Sales Rep 1, and second, although the close percentage for Unpaid is higher, the average and total revenues are much, much lower. Sales Rep 1 has an average contract of $39,576.96 for Unpaid Advertising, and Sales Rep 2 has an average contract of only $6,116.63. Sales Rep 1 total revenues for Unpaid Advertising is $672,808.30, and for Sales Rep 2 it is only $116,102.00. Why is there the huge discrepancy? Again, this should be examined and hopefully changes can be made which will result in improvement moving forward.

Graph 7

Sales Rep 1	# of Leads	# of Closes	Revenue	Closing %	Ad Cost	Ad Cost % of Sales	Avg. Contract	Avg. Cost/Sale
Paid	81	17	$466,346.80	21.0%	$47,884.99	10.27%	$27,432.16	$2,816.76
Unpaid	47	17	$672,808.30	36.2%	$0.00	0.00%	$39,576.96	$0.00
Totals	128	34	$1,139,155.10	26.6%	$47,884.99	4.20%	$33,504.56	$1,408.38

Sales Rep 2	# of Leads	# of Closes	Revenue	Closing %	Ad Cost	Ad Cost % of Sales	Avg. Contract	Avg. Cost/Sale
Paid	90	23	$765,233.00	25.6%	$67,270.00	8.79%	$33,271.00	$2,924.78
Unpaid	30	19	$116,102.00	63.3%	$0.00	0.00%	$6,110.63	$0.00
Totals	120	42	$881,335.00	35.0%	$67,270.00	7.63%	$20,984.17	$1,601.67

There are so many ways you can look at this data and manipulate it, and it all plays a part somewhere, but for planning sales and marketing for your company, we will focus now on the cost of getting a sale in percent and dollars, both by individual sales rep and by company averages, and the number of leads required to reach goal. (Graph 7) For Sales Rep 1, it costs on average 4.2% of his sales. For Sales Rep 2, it costs about 7.63% of his sales.

Now that all the data for the individual sales reps is gathered, then put it all together as a company, as shown below in Graph 8.

Graph 8

Company Totals	# of Leads	# of Closes	Revenue	Closing %	Ad Cost	Ad Cost % of Sales	Avg. Contract	Avg. Cost/Sale
Paid	171	40	$1,231,579.80	23.3%	$115,154.99	9.03%	$30,864.50	$2,787.06
Unpaid	77	36	$788,910.30	46.7%	$0.00	0.00%	$21,914.17	$0.00
Totals	248	76	$2,020,490.10	30.1%	$115,154.99	5.6%	$26,585.40	$1,488.78

We have most of our preliminary numbers, but there's one more. That is the cost of getting a lead. I wrote about the cost of getting a sale, but not necessarily the cost of getting a lead.

Look at Graph 9. We are only going to consider lead cost. The way I came up with the average cost per lead was taking the total cost of Paid Advertising and dividing it by the number of Paid Advertising leads received last year. That's $115,154.99 divided by 171 to get $673.42.

Graph 9: Lead Cost Analysis

Company Totals	# of Leads	Total Ad Cost	Avg. Cost/Lead
Paid	171	$115,154.99	$673.42
Unpaid	77	$0.00	$0.00
Totals	370	$115,154.99	$382.21

Now let's consider all the Company Totals for Sales and Marketing Projections.

The numbers in Graph 10 below are the numbers that will be used to plan my company sales and marketing goals. I will go back to the individual sales rep numbers when the sales reps plan their personal goals.

History is going to be used to repeat itself, or at least the parts of history that are beneficial! Yes, history does repeat itself unless some changes are made, and as we saw, there are some changes that will need to be made in order to reach the sales goals that were set for the coming year.

At any rate, you can use your history to predict your future.

First of all, you need to know your company goals and put together a budget. Where do you want your company revenues to be a year from now? Once you know that, and if your profit margins are staying the same, you can set your sales goals and marketing budget.

Using percentages from the historical data in Graph 8, start to fill in the Sales Goal Projections Chart.

Graph 10: Sales Goal Projections Chart

	Leads	Avg. Closing %	Closes	Avg. Contract	Projected Sales
Paid		23.3%		$30,864.50	
Unpaid		43%		$21,914.17	
TOTAL GOAL					**$3,000,000.00**

The sales goal is $3,000,000.00. The average closing percentage and the average contract dollars are all filled in.

Before continuing from this point, you need to know how many dollars in sales you want to come from Paid Advertising and how many from Unpaid Advertising. In looking over the data, it seemed very viable that we could really work individually and as a company to really mine our database and find good reasons to get back in front of previous customers and either work with them or get referrals to help improve on this. We have felt that we needed to take conscious steps to generate more leads from Unpaid Advertising.

We decided to split it evenly. The goal was to get just as many revenues from Unpaid Advertising as we wanted from Paid.

Our thought was that if we could make a certain number of sales at our historical average dollar amount, we would meet our company goals. Our tracking history also showed an interesting point in that as the number of Paid Leads increased for the sales people, their closing ratios decreased. Where is the happy medium that would help our sales people reach their goals, help the company reach its goal, and not leave a lot of wasted leads and money on the table simply because a sales rep had too many leads to work diligently and effectively?

In order to reach our increased sales goal, we needed more sales people. Our strategy was that if we increased the size of the sales team, there would be more people in the team among which to spread those averages proportionately, and we knew that we could depend at least on the Law of Averages to bring in what was required to meet our company goal.

How many leads do we need? Let's fill in the chart to find out.

Graph 11: It's time for Backwards Math! Step-By-Step Planning

	Leads	Avg. Closing %	Closes	Avg. Contract	Projected Sales
Paid		23.3%		$30,864.50	$1,500,000.00
Unpaid		43%		$21,914.17	$1,500,000.00
TOTAL GOAL					**$3,000,000.00**

1. Start off by filling in the empty spaces with $1,500,000 for the Projected Sales for both Paid and Unpaid Advertising. (Some of the numbers will be rounded for simplicity's sake.)

2. Now divide $1,500,000 by the average contract size of $30,864 for Paid Advertising, and you'll get 48.60. Round it

up and that means the company will need 49 closed sales of approximately $30,864.

3. Take the 49 closes and divide it by the closing percentage of 23.3%, and you will get 210. The company will need 210 Paid Advertising Leads.

Graph 12: Filling in the empty spaces

	Leads	Avg. Closing %	Closes	Avg. Contract	Projected Sales
Paid	210	23.3%	49	$30,864.50	$1,500,000.00
Unpaid		43%		$21,914.17	$1,500,000.00
TOTAL GOAL					$3,000,000.00

Now fill in the Unpaid Advertising lines in the same way.

4. Divide $1,500,000 by the average contract size of $21,914 for Unpaid Advertising and you'll get 68.44. Round it up and that means the company will need 69 closed sales of approximately $21,914.

5. Take the 69 closes and divide it by the closing percentage of 43%, and you will get 160. The company will need 160 Unpaid Advertising Leads.

Graph 13: Continuing to fill in Unpaid Advertising.

Sales Rep 2	Leads	Avg. Closing %	Closes	Avg. Contract	Projected Sales
Paid	210	23.3%	49	$30,864.50	$1,500,000.00
Unpaid	160	43%	69	$21,914.17	$1,500,000.00
Totals					**$3,000,000.00**

Combining Paid and Unpaid Advertising, the company will need 370 leads during the coming year to reach your company goal.

Graph 14: Your total leads required

	Leads	Avg. Closing %	Closes	Avg. Contract	Projected Sales
Paid	210	23.3%	49	$30,864.50	$1,500,000.00
Unpaid	160	43%	69	$21,914.17	$1,500,000.00
TOTAL GOAL	370				**$3,000,000.00**

Now if we go back to the cost per lead and plug in the numbers of the average cost and multiply it by 210, you will see that it comes nowhere near the $300,000 that is allotted in my marketing budget.

Graph 15: Total Cost Per Lead

Take 210 leads and multiply it by $673.42 to come up with $141,418.20. $141,418.20 is a far cry from the $300,000 that my 10% marketing budget allows.

Company Totals	# of Leads	Total Ad Cost	Avg. Cost/Lead
Paid	210	$141,418.20	$673.42
Unpaid	160	$0.00	$0.00
Totals	370	$141,418.20	$382.21

Take 210 leads and multiply it by $673.42 to come up with $141,418.20. $141,418.20 is a far cry from the $300,000 that my 10% marketing budget allows.

That is okay. That is a good position to be in. Not every dollar has to be pinned immediately to an advertising campaign. It is nice when there is wiggle room in the marketing budget, because it allows opportunities to play around a bit and try new advertising campaigns.

When you try those new tactics, though, have this Average Lead Cost as a reference point as to what your typical Paid Advertising leads have cost. Although you will want to keep an eye on this number, it is more important to follow the progress of those leads, and if they turn to profitable sales, it does not matter how much money is spent on that advertising! (One thing I tell marketers is that the sky is the limit for what can be paid, as long as the advertising cost is bringing in sales at a volume that are profitable. My goal is to partner with those from whom I buy advertising, and work together in order to really make their advertising work.)

If you do not want to add more advertising campaigns to your marketing, that is fine. With the way it is set up then, in the example above, you should not need $300,000 to get your expected results. If that money is not spent on advertising campaigns, it just goes to the bottom line in Profits, and you dropped your cost of sale percentage.

So what is the most important bottom number I need to watch?

The number of leads you get.

This company needs 370 leads to reach its goal. Divide 370 by 52, and the company will need approximately seven leads a week. Don't leave the office on Friday until there are seven leads for the following week.

In this case, the $3 Million Dollar process begins by making sure there are seven leads a week. If that happens, and those leads are followed up on as diligently as before, they will be on target to reach or even exceed their goal.

It all boils down to a single digit. Incredible, isn't it? Just seven leads a week.

How do I get all these numbers together?

In years past, before the advent of software programs, people who wanted to run their businesses or grow profitably tracked these numbers by hand. So did we. Yes, it was cumbersome, and yes, we had to hire people specifically for these tracking purposes. They tracked with paper and pencil until Excel came along, and we used that, too.

For our businesses, it seemed a rather costly way to get the numbers, but we knew full well that the cost we would pay in lost revenues was far greater than the cost of an assistant to track the numbers. We knew we needed these numbers in order to drive our sales and marketing in a way we wanted them to go.

Finally, we automated all of this when we developed Profit Finder Pro Software, so now we have all this information immediately available to us with a few clicks of the mouse.

Whether you use paper and pencil or a software system, having these numbers can make a difference between your business barely surviving or thriving.

How will you do it? You will need to have the tools to monitor, and the understanding to know whether or not certain advertising is working for you. When your systems are in place, if someone is in charge of making absolute sure that there are the pre-determined number of leads each week, you will reach your goal.

Questions for Your Business:

1. What is your goal for gross revenues in the coming year?
2. Using past history, how many leads will you need to reach your goal?
3. How many dollars do you expect to come from unpaid vs. paid advertising?
4. How many leads will you need from unpaid advertising? Paid?
5. Do you have a system in place to make sure each sales rep is on track for getting the proper number of leads required in order to reach the revenues they are aiming for?
6. Do you have a system in place that will show you that each sales rep is on track as expected for the number of closes, average revenues generated, and is within their expected margins for bringing in sales profitably?

NOTES

Chapter 9

Helping Your Sales Reps Plan for Success

As business owners, we want our Sales people to be successful. Their success means our success, and as long as they are successful, they generally will stay with us. It is so much more pleasant and financially rewarding to be able to keep productive sales people working with a company for longer periods of time. Things seem to run more smoothly, and once people are in tune to how the company runs, they settle in and start to focus on making money.

On the other hand, constant turnover is exasperating and hard on a company. Not only is it expensive, but it decreases morale, and it just seems that a business can never start working like a well-greased wheel when it always has to start and stop to train new people.

The goal should be to work with sales people, and provide them an opportunity to create their own "business-inside-a-business", so to speak. Let them set their own goals and have control over how much money they want to make, and allow them a lot of room to move about as long as they stay within certain boundaries (most importantly, profit margins) of the company. If their goal is to make money, they are likely an immediate kindred spirit, because that is the reason people are in business. In fact, if you are interviewing, and ask what a prospective sales person compensation requirements are, and they want to settle for salary, raise your eyebrows and ask, "Really?" And pay attention to the answer. It's telling.

When somebody is on board your bus, what can you do to help them be successful from a sales and marketing standpoint? How can you use their history to help them plan? Just as your company plans its sales and marketing goals, your sales reps, too, need to use their history to help them plan for their own "business-inside-a-business" plan.

In the previous chapter, I showed some graphs with individual sales reps' data. They will use this same type of data to help them plan for their success. For them, too, it's going to boil down to a single number that they will focus on weekly in order to reach their sales goal success.

Look at Sales Rep 1 again.

Graph 1: Sales Data from Last Year.

Sales Rep 1	# of Leads	# of Closes	Closing %	Avg. Contract	Revenue
Paid	81	17	21.0%	$27,432.16	$466,346.80
Unpaid	47	17	36.2%	$39,576.96	$672,808.30
Totals	128	34	26.6%	$33,504.56	$1,139,155.10

Last year his sales were $1,139,155.10. In the coming year he plans to bring those sales to $1,300,000. What is needed?

Well, first of all, the company is going to provide him with 104 Paid Advertising leads in the coming year, as long as he continues to close at an acceptable rate and volume.

Based on history, we start with these numbers, and will use them to help plan for next year:

Graph 2

Now let's fill in his chart by doing "Backwards Math" again!

Sales Rep 1	# of Leads	# of Closes	Closing %	Avg. Contract	Revenue
Paid	104		21.0%	$27,432.16	
Unpaid			36.2%	$39,576.96	
Totals				$33,504.56	$1,300,000.00

Graph 3

Sales Rep 1	# of Leads	# of Closes	Closing %	Avg. Contract	Revenue
Paid	104	22	21.0%	$27,432.16	$603,507.52
Unpaid	50	18	36.2%	$39,576.96	$696,492.48
Totals	154	40	26%	$32,500.00	$1,300,000.00

He is being offered 104 Paid leads. His average closing rate is 21.0%, so:

- Multiply 104 by 21.0% to equal 21.84. Round up to get 22. He will close 22 leads.
- Multiply the 22 sales by his average contract size of $27,432.16 to get $603,507.52. That is the amount of revenue he can plan on coming in through Paid Advertising if he keeps his average closing ratio and contract amount as they have been.
- Now subtract $603,507.52 from $1,300,000.00 to get $696,492.48 in Revenues he needs to generate from Unpaid Advertising in order to reach his goal.

- Take the Revenues of $696,492.48 and divide it by the Average Contract of $39,576.96 for Unpaid Advertising to get the number of sales he will need from Unpaid Advertising. You will get 17.5. Round it up to 18.
- Take the 18 sales and divide it by his closing rate of 36.2% to get 49.72. Round it up. He will need approximately 50 Unpaid Advertising leads in order to close at his average rate and reach his goal.
- Add the number of Total Closes to get 40. Divide 40 by 154 to get his Total Average Closing Ratio of 26%.
- Divide his Total Revenues by 40 to get his Average Contract size of $32,500.00.
- Add the Paid and Unpaid Lead together to get 154. Sales Rep 1 needs 154 leads in order to reach his goal.
- Divide 154 by 52. Sales Rep 1 needs 3 leads per week in order to reach his goal.

Although the company has committed to providing 104 leads, since your sales rep is still the one who will ultimately want to be in control of how much he or she makes, he will want to make sure to track to see that he is indeed getting the required number of leads and closing at an appropriate level in order to stay on track with both Paid and Unpaid Advertising for reaching his goal.

If it happens that the company runs out of leads, is he really going to allow that to affect his income? Hopefully not! Regardless of where the leads are coming from, it is in his best interests to make sure the pipeline stays filled, and get his 3 qualified leads each week. That is the only dependable way of reaching his goal.

If he follows these numbers, he will reach his goal.

Now that you have worked through the steps, know that you do not have to do the manual math for every sales rep in your company. There are faster ways to figure this out. On one of my website pages I have a Sales Goal Calculator, and it will do all the figuring for you as long as you know how much you want to make, your average job size, average closing ratio, commission percentage and the amount of time you have to reach that goal. It will let you know the exact number of leads you need down to the day. Just go to http://www.ProfitFinderPro.com/sales-goal-calculator.

You know the numbers, so then what?

So now that you know how to help a sales rep set their goals down to the very number of leads they need each week, how can you help them reach their goal? What else can be done?

Not only do we want to work with them in setting their individual goals, but we want to help them create a plan in which they can reach those goals. We really need to want to partner with our sales reps, and have a friendly relationship that allows them to ask questions and bounce thoughts and ideas off you. A great sales rep will always be open to other people's input and ideas, too, as long as it helps him improve. Remember, their success means the company's success.

There are definite ways to help sales reps increase their closing ratios and revenues, and this is a great time to review their strengths and weaknesses. What are the strong points that they can focus on in order to benefit their sales? Are there areas that can be improved? How can you help them succeed? What can you do in your sales training to help them close at a higher rate or volume? What are the success areas of some of your sales people that could be shared with the others as a way to learn? How can you help instill in them the importance of keeping in touch with their previous customers?

Talk with your sales people. Set measureable goals and checkpoints that are agreeable to both them and the company. How will you measure their progress? What tools and systems are you providing that allows your sales reps to be able to keep an eye on the numbers?

When you have the numbers in front of you, they start to tell a story. Pay attention, be inquisitive, and take action.

It all comes down to the numbers, and the action taken based on those numbers.

Winners really do know their numbers.

Questions for Your Business:

1. Is there anything in the way you run your business that hinders your salesperson's success? If so, what can be done about that?

2. Do you have a lot of turnover in your business that's indicative of a leadership problem? Why?

3. Is your whole team "on the bus?" If not, why are they there?

4. Do you allow your salespeople room to be their own "business-within-your-business" as long as they perform within certain expectations?

5. What can you do to help your people be the best they can be?

NOTES

Chapter 10

More Suggestions for Using Data

I kind of covered the main points about sales and marketing that I wanted to make in this book, and if you were to do nothing more than what has been explained, you will see a dramatic increase, especially if you are doing no tracking currently. Guaranteed. However, if you are already tracking and you have the data, there are a few more simple things you can do with that data to help increase revenues.

Your customer database is a goldmine if it is set up in a way that can be used. This is something that should be used for all your mailing lists, scheduling, maintenance, and other types of follow up. It is a continuous work in progress, and something that has to be continuously maintained because it is only as good as the data that is in it.

Nurturing to the Point of Sale

If a person comes in as a prospect instead of a viable lead, mark it as that and keep working it. For example, at trade shows and expos there are so many people coming through, and some of them are probably stronger candidates for your product or service than others. Mark their records in a way so that you can get to those ones faster.

This is an example of a way that worked for one company to nurture prospects to a qualified lead. This was a home improvement company that sold high-end remodeling. They put a booth in a beautiful, huge display center that was set in the middle of an exclusive geographic area, a prime residential for doing business. Homeowners from around the area would come, give their contact information of at least a phone number or email address, state their purpose of visiting, and then walk through at their leisure. The booths were unmanned, with the exception of one evening and one Saturday a month. The purpose was to let them walk through without having to *fear* sales pitches. (I say that half-smiling.) If they were interested in a certain company, they would scan a barcode and then that information would be transferred to the front desk. A packet of information regarding each of those companies was waiting for them by the time they finished their tour of the building.

Each company was notified at the end of each day and given the contact information of every person who scanned the barcode on their booth. Now it was up to the company to follow up.

Within a couple weeks, the company had a pile of papers with a list of names on each paper. They called or tried calling everyone at least once, but in many cases, did not make contact. When the person did not pick up the phone, the sales rep often didn't follow up, and the connection between the prospective customers and company had not been made.

As time went on, this place became more popular, and more and more people were going through. At the same time, the pile on the contractor's desk was growing, notes were getting scattered, and it was turning into more of a headache than it seemed to be worth. So many calls were made and it seemed so seldom that anyone was answering the phone or, if they did answer, they were not interested in getting an estimate.

Well, the business owner who had a beautiful, expensive display there was getting disenchanted, and was becoming less and less inclined to even follow up on the calls...until it hit someone that this was insane! All these people who were somewhat interested in their services actually scanned their code and wanted more information about the company. These were real prospects!

What they ended up doing was setting up a prospecting system within their database, and every name that came in was entered into that system. When a call was made, if an appointment was not made at that moment, a note was made in the history and the calendar was marked for the next follow-up date. There were times when they made contact with homeowners who said they were just browsing and trying to get ideas for when they start remodeling next year. Well, the calendar was marked for a few months ahead of whenever "next year" was, and these people were put on the mailing list.

They also had a great brochure they offered to send the people, as a way to legitimately ask for their mailing addresses, if those were missing. Those people were now in the loop of their marketing system. The calendars were marked for phone calls to be made, and the history told the story of their previous conversations or attempts at making touch.

And then they followed through. When they made that initial call, there were many times they had to leave a message, and the wording of that message was well scripted. They would say something like, "I'm following up on your request to contact you through the Display Center. I just wanted to touch base with you and see what you had in mind for your project. Since you asked me to call, I

> *Then they followed through.*

really want to make sure we connect, so if I don't hear back within a couple days, I'll call again until I get in touch with you. If you are not interested, that's fine. Just let me know, please, because I certainly do not mean to bother you with my calls."

Do you think they had a good return on their calls? They most certainly did, because if the prospect did not call back, the scheduler had marked the calendar to call back as promised, and they followed through. If the prospect was interested they called back. If they did not want to keep getting the calls, they called back. Either way, the company was able to make the connection. Some of them took at least seven or eight calls, plus a couple letters or emails, and *still* converted to sales! But the time involved was very minimal because it was so systematized. In the end, this center ended up being very profitable for the company. They had hundreds of thousands of dollars in sales from those leads.

When I found out what was happening with this particular business, and saw how, after a few month's time, they were suddenly able to convert their prospects to viable leads and then sales, I went to visit the center. In walking through I saw that some businesses had pulled their booths, and I was concerned for a couple reasons: 1) several of my clients had booths in there, and 2) if other businesses would start to pull their booths, this would not be good advertisement for the Display Center and the flow of people would likely slow down, which would then affect my customers, too.

I made an appointment to speak with the owner, because I knew that if he would give me the floor and a voice, I could help all those 250 other businesses that had booths housed there. Now remember, I am a tracking expert, and I know that tracking will increase revenues. Because of this other business's experience and speaking with my other customers who had display booths there, I had a pretty strong hunch of what was going on. Coming from a background of small business, I also recognized the golden opportunity for those who were proactive while others sat back. Unfortunately, the owner of the design center did not recognize the need, and did not foresee the domino effect of businesses pulling out. In short order, that center was closed down.

I ended up contacting quite a few of the business owners that had left. They pretty much all gave the same reason for leaving: they were not making sales. They had piles of papers full of names, but were never able to reach the people, so they just quit calling after one attempt. The papers piled up on their desk or in their email. Pretty soon it got to the point where they did not even make an attempt to call, just like the company I told you about a bit ago. Feeble excuse, I know, but it was true. It was too much hassle. I understood; they did not have a way to easily track what was going on. There was no method to the madness, they had no follow up system, and in the end they just gave up. Just think, these were the very same leads that several of my clients followed through on, and made hundreds of thousands of dollars in sales.

In my mind, that center would never have had to close, and the other businesses could have made profitable sales just like my clients did if they'd had their systems in place. Guess what else! Those clients of mine are still getting calls as a result of that display center that closed down a couple years ago. The names, addresses, and email addresses of these prospects that were put into the system as long as three and a half years ago are getting regular contact, and as a result, sales are still being made.

All because of a system that is in place.

Rehashing Old Leads

Earlier I mentioned that when a person calls for an estimate or expresses an interest in whatever it is you are selling, the likelihood of them buying right away is maybe about 30%. This rate depends on your industry, of course, but let's just say you sell higher ticket items. Of those who do not buy now, 60% of them will buy from *someone* within a year. Wouldn't it be nice to be that *someone*?

Varying somewhat by the cost or investment of money for the service or product you are selling, it may take up to two years for the people who do not buy now to buy from *someone*. If you are on top of your game, and have a good follow-up system in place, that means you may be that *someone*, and your company closing percentage or ratio will increase; it is just that there will be a delay on some of those closes.

So look back at this example. Your company closed 1 out of 3. That means if you closed approximately 60 now, there are 120 that have not closed, and from those, 72 will buy within the year. If you are persistent and keep in front of those 72 prospects, there is a possibility of closing perhaps another 23 leads (33% of 72). What is your average sale in dollars? Imagine what this could do to help your bottom line, especially if you have higher ticket items. Unfortunately, if there is not a follow up system in place, these closing percentages tend to drop over longer periods of time simply because the leads are not followed up on. The fact of the matter, though, is that you still have a great chance at more sales if you have a follow-up system in place! Front of mind, front of mind, front of mind. You always want to be in that position with your customers.

There are statistics available that show the rate of delayed buying according to industry, so find out what it is for your industry. That will give you a better idea of how often and for how long you need to be in touch with these people.

Communication and keeping good records is so important for the sake of rehashing those old leads that do not convert right away. If the customer is not buying, they may or may not tell you why, but if you do not ask, it is a sure thing that you will not know. Sometimes they may even say one thing, but that does not always give the real picture either. Listen to what they say, and hear what they do not say! No matter what it is, when they give a reason, make a note of it. If they are looking for something down the road, make a note of it. Mark your calendar; it only takes a few seconds to make the entry.

> *L*isten to what customers say, and hear what they do not!

This happened in one of our companies recently. As part of their process, they have someone go through and follow up on appointments after a certain amount of time that the lead is still open. Then, based on that conversation, that person will either mark the record as dead or leave it open and keep working it.

In going through the records, they pull up the flags for the day. One of these flags was for a prospective customer for whom one of their reps had gone and given an estimate for $35,000 three years before. In the records it was noted that these people said the company's price was "higher than a kite", so they were not going with them. Well, the person who flagged the record realized that these particular people really seemed to want to do the project, and they had certain expectations, wants, and desires, and it seemed they had the money to do it. Knowing that, they figured that the people would have called a few others for estimates, and probably found that everyone was coming in around the same price, but those prices were higher than they had expected, and so now they had to rethink their finances. These people had been on the mailing lists, had gotten monthly emails, and the company name was still familiar and in front of them.

Fast forward in time: the prospects were poking around the emails, opening links, looking at pictures on the website. Great! Now it was time to call again. One call confirmed that no, they had not done their project, and yes, they were still wanting to do it. Sure, they would like to set another appointment and re-visit the conversation. Long story short, they ended up signing a $99,000 contract, nearly three times what the original estimate had been three years earlier. All because someone listened and took note, and subsequently set the calendar to follow up. And they are a delighted, happy customer. It is hard to get better than having a customer smile as they write a nice check like that, right?

If this kind of thing happened only once, I would not call it the rule. But when it happens over and over again, and often enough to make it worth it, it is called a rule. Make sure you have a way to go after those possibilities for people who have expressed an interest, but do not buy immediately. Many of them will buy eventually, and if you are constantly at the front of their minds, you are likely the one they will choose.

Customer Maintenance and Repeat Sales

Once you have marketed to get a customer, why not keep them for life? Why not sell to them twice? Or three times? Or more? The purpose of paying for marketing up front is so that your marketing can pay for you later. In other words, why should you always have to work so hard and pay so much to constantly acquire new customers? At some point, if you have taken care of your customers, they should start taking care of you through either repeat business or referrals. Why spend so much time, energy, and money by always having to bring in new customers? If you do not have a reason to go back and sell another product or service, invent one. These people are ready customers, ready to buy from you because your company served them well the first time.

If you have a service-related business, put them on a maintenance plan and offer a quarterly, bi-annual or annual service. Upon completion of one service, you should be marking your records to call them or send a notification for another sale down the road exactly two years or three months or six months or whatever the predetermined time is that you can legitimately go out and offer more services.

For example, if you are a dentist, send an email or letter or make a phone call once every six months to come in for cleaning. If you are a tree-trimming service, send out the fall and spring cleanup letters to all who have previously used your service. If you are a chiropractor, you certainly have ample opportunity for a monthly maintenance program. If you have a spa, if they do not sign on for a recurring charge for your monthly service, at least give them a call every quarter. If you are a roofer, consider the timeline of when maintenance and re-sealing needs to be done around the chimneys and pipes. If it is two years from the date of installation, send a letter or call them after two years and say your records show their roof is due for maintenance. In order to extend your warranty, please call us to set a time for one of our people to come out. Pest Control, HVAC Maintenance, Window Sealing, Foam Roof Recoating, Interior and Exterior Painting, Pool Deck Sealing, Carpet Cleaners. You name it, the list is endless. Every business should have a way to get back in front of their customers.

Think of the last time you needed a carpet cleaner or a glass replacement company. By the next time you needed them, did you have their number on hand? Did you remember their company name? I think every time I have needed a windshield replaced I use a different company because I can never remember who I used before. Same with carpet cleaners. Do not wait for your customers to call. People's lives are busy and, believe it or not, even if you told them at the point of sale that they should call back in five years for maintenance, they will not remember to call, and in some cases they will not even remember the name of *who* to call!

Why not pick up the phone? These people know you, they trust you, like you, and would like you to be the one to continue on with the maintenance of whatever it is you offer instead of always switching from one to the next. It is automatic jingle in your pockets!

Mailing Lists

In your customer database you should have really quick and easy access to find the contacts for any type of a mailing list, whether it be snail mail, email, or text messages. You should be able to filter through a variety of tags and pull any targeted list at any given time.

Having this ease is really important. Laona lives in Wyoming, but takes the calls and does the marketing for a Phoenix-based property investment company. Since their system is set up over the internet, geographic location does not matter. She said that once they got their system in place, it became so much easier to search contacts looking for specific properties by typing key words into the search bar! It is so much easier to pull lists when the data is in an organized system instead of having to scroll through endless Excel sheets or address books.

You see, time is of the essence to these people. When a property comes up for sale or an investor is inquiring about buying, they need to be able to get in contact with the interested parties and properties as quickly as possible.

Another example of a business owner using his lead tracking system to his benefit when time was of the essence was a roofing business who tapped into his database within half an hour of a horrendous hail storm that pummeled its way through Scottsdale, AZ. First of all, he sent emails out to all of his existing customers whose roofs they had completed in certain ZIP codes, because he knew a large number of shingle and foam roofs in the line of that storm were more than likely trashed.

Then he sent another email to the homeowners whose roofs they had looked at but not sold. If those people had not bought from someone else, they would have some serious roof leaks because even the sturdiest roofs had not held up in that storm. After sending the emails out, he sent a regular postal letter to each homeowner. Needless to say, by the time all was said and done, it was a multi-million dollar storm for his company. Not only was he able to be the hero and run to the rescue of his current clients, but he was able to offer his services once again to those whom he had already met and were now in a position of real need. He was able to get in front of his customers quickly because he had a fast and easy way to pull that data and get back to the people who mattered in that instant.

Another really important reason to contact parts of your database is when one of your sales reps leaves, be it for whatever reason. As in anything else, there are times when our paths part. Whether or not it was on friendly terms, it would be good to let the prospects and customers who were working with that salesperson know that "Sales Rep A is no longer with our company; however Sales Rep B is going to carry on where Sales Rep A left off. If you are waiting on something from Sales Rep A, please call our office right away. Otherwise please expect a call from Sales Rep B in the coming days so that he can introduce himself."

Not only is that another touch in front of the customer, but there have been times when Sales Rep A has not left on the best of terms, and it is always in the best interests of the company to be the first to tell the customers. The sooner, the better.

In the recent past, fewer and fewer people have been using direct mail. I'm sure part of the reason is because of cost; it's much cheaper to send email than it is to send direct mail. However, if you take a look at the open rate of email, you will probably see that a large percentage of your emails are not being opened. 25% is considered a really good open rate. That means 75 out of 100 are not seeing your messages! Sure, it's cheaper, but think of all the people who never see your message! What does it matter how cheap the marketing is if the message does not get through, right?

> *Wh*at does it matter how cheap the marketing is if the message does not get through?

Seeing this over and over again, we started segmenting our lists. If emails were consistently opened, great. If not, they went on the snail mail list. The 75% who were not seeing the emails were now seeing direct mail in their mailboxes. Of course we still send emails to 100% of our email list, because there is nothing to lose, but when we send direct mail, we pay a little more attention. There are times when we sent a direct mail piece to our entire list, but certainly not as frequently as emails. We have also found that once we start sending direct mail, the open rate of those otherwise-unopened emails has started to increase to some extent. I suppose it is because frequency begets familiarity, and when a person starts to recognize you more often, they start to pay attention. Once they start to pay attention, then the message starts to be delivered, which then leads to a sale.

Again, when you can set up your system to "tag and flag" your people in certain ways, this whole process does not have to be cumbersome. It just helps you deliver the message to the people who are needing or waiting for your service in a way that is meaningful to them.

There are so many different reasons and ways to pull marketing lists. Sometimes you may be giving special offers at different times, so you want to market to certain lists. Sometimes you may be sending Christmas or holiday cards at the end of the year. Who knows, the reasons are endless as to why you could be sending out mailers, but the whole point is, make sure your system allows you quick and easy access to get them in whatever manner you want or need!

Questions for Your Business:

1. How many times do you reach out in some way or another to each prospective client before they become a customer?
2. What type of system do you have set up so that you have an easy way to follow up on previous leads or prospects?
3. What happens when a lead becomes DEAD? Do you mark your records to differentiate the type of follow up you may have with them? When and how do you REHASH those leads?
4. Does your business have a reason to get back in front of previous customers for repeat business? If not, what legitimate service could you offer in order to get back in front of them?
5. When an opportunity arises for a letter or email to go out, how do you sort and filter your mailing lists quickly for the desired recipients?

NOTES

Chapter 11

Sales and Marketing Numbers Any Business Owner Should Know

Toward the beginning of this book, I mentioned the four questions that have been at the top of business owners' minds, and the four things that keep them awake at night.

1. How can I get more customers (generate new sales) and keep the ones I already have?
2. How can I keep expenses from eating my profits?
3. How can I keep a positive cash flow?
4. How can I grow my business?

The answer to all four of these questions is, track it to crack it! Winners know their numbers, there is no doubt about it. Take a close and honest look at your business. Are you able to keep your finger on the pulse of business, especially the profit-making areas? Do you have quick and easy access to your data? Are you able to manipulate it into a usable fashion so that your sales and marketing decisions are based on facts instead of gut feelings? Do you have an easy way for your sales and marketing people to have access to the information that they can affect and affects them? Any winner wants to see their numbers. Have them available.

Throughout this book I have illustrated different data to track that will effectively answer all of these questions and guide you and your business toward intentional growth and success. Do not underestimate the power of your sales and marketing data. This is not all inclusive, but even if you only knew *these* numbers, your business could grow in ways you never imagined!

Are you ready to grow?

This is a brief list of the numbers you should know in order to improve Salesperson effectiveness:

- Individual salesperson closing ratio per lead source
- Closing ratio in comparison to industry averages, company standards, and goals
- Cost of leads sold per individual salesperson
- Contract size by salesperson in comparison with company averages
- Gross profits on dollars sold including the cost of the lead
- Numbers of sales for self-generated, previous customers, or referral business (unpaid advertising)
- Individual salesperson strengths and weaknesses in company product line

This is a brief list of the numbers you should know in order to improve Marketing effectiveness:

- Number and cost of leads received per advertising source
- Types of leads per source
- Number of leads that converted to sales
- Actual company profitability of sales from any lead source
- Percentage of total dollars in sales versus total dollars spent in advertising
- Lead conversion timetable: leads to sales to billable sales
- Types of leads & sales coming from each market and geographical locations

Hopefully, by this time you have a clearer picture of the type of system necessary to give you the numbers you need to run and grow your business profitably. By knowing these numbers and maybe doing even a few of the suggestions as described in the book, all four of the questions that keep business owners awake at night will have been answered. However, to know and to take action are two completely different things. A person can know all they want, but it is of no benefit unless action is taken. It is far more fun and exciting to be an active one. It is especially fun when those actions start bringing in results.

Winners Know Their Numbers.

Questions for Your Business:

1. Considering the lists of numbers a business owner should know as described in this chapter, what numbers do you know?
2. Considering the lists of numbers a business owner should know as described in this chapter, what numbers do you NOT know?
3. How could knowing the numbers you DO NOT know help increase revenues?
4. Answer the Four Questions as stated:
    A. How can I get more customers (generate new sales) and keep the ones I already have?
    B. How can I keep Expenses from eating my Profits?
    C. How can I keep a positive cash flow?
    D. How can I grow my business?

NOTES

Chapter 12

Wrapping It All Up

How Many Leads Do I Need To Reach My Goal?

Part of this is a repeat from the end of Chapter 9, but it is the starting point of reaching goals, so it's important enough to repeat. The number of leads a business or salesperson needs to reach his or her sales goal is determined by company and individual averages. If you have been tracking, you can get a quick idea of how many leads it takes to make a sale, the conversion time, and the dollars generated. History helps plan for the future, and the numbers play out in such a predictable fashion.

The first step is to know how much money the company or a sales rep wants to make during any given time. Plug that number into a sales goal calculator (www.ProfitFinderPro.com/sales-goal-calculator), enter the length of time you have to earn it, the average contract amount and average closing percentage.

This will spit out the number of leads you need each day, week and month in order to reach your monthly, quarterly, or yearly goals.

Knowing how many leads are required in order to meet a monthly, quarterly or annual goal is important on a couple different levels. First of all, the business owners needs to know in order to plan a marketing budget. How much money has it typically cost to get a lead? What does it cost to get a sale? How much, then, can you plan to spend in order to get the dollar volume you need?

For myself, I'm constantly looking at the ad campaigns going on, the number of dollars spent, and the number of leads that have come in. If I have spent a bunch of money on some advertising and no leads are coming in, you can be sure that I'm talking with those advertising people until either the leads start coming in or we cut the advertising. At the same time, I'm working my leads from other advertising to offset the higher cost of this advertising that does not appear to be working at the time. I'm on the teeter-totter; it is all a balancing act again. I know that I have so long to get a certain number of leads, and if that does not come in, I am not going to reach my goal. So it goes; the quest for leads is continuous. If I take care of getting the leads in the door, the rest will be okay.

Then secondly, a salesperson wants and needs to know how many leads they need in order to reach his or her goal. By knowing this, they have total control over their earnings. If their goal is a million dollars and they know that in order to reach a million dollars, they need to have at least one appointment every day, then it is up to them to make sure they have that appointment. The motivated sales rep will make sure of it, and will not allow the company or the sales manager to control his or her earnings.

By this I mean, if the company has not been able to provide enough leads for him to reach his goal, he will get them himself because he knows that in order to reach his goal, he has to have at least one appointment a day. He is diligent to get back to previous customers to ask for repeat business or referrals, and he's out there networking and making working relationships. Before he leaves work on Friday or Saturday, his calendar is filled to its required fullness for the following week. Before he leaves for vacation, he has double-booked some days to make up for time that he is away. He knows exactly what is required to meet the goal, and will do all within his power to reach it.

This year I worked with a company who had a salesperson that had fallen behind goal. I did some quick math based on what was projected at the end of last year, and determined that if that person had been diligently doing exactly as the sales goal calculator told him, he would be right on track. His average close rate and sale size were the same, but he did not have enough leads. He depended on the company to provide all those, which they did not provide, and then sat back and wondered why he was not on track to reach his goal.

Winners know their numbers *and then take action.* Even when it comes to getting the required number of leads.

Do Customers Call Your Office
to Set Appointments?

Are you a service-oriented company that puts your phone number in your advertising so people can call to set an On-location appointment for your product or service? If so, do you have someone answering the phone, getting all the information you need, and setting the appointments or consultations? If not, why?

Think of the times you personally make calls to set an appointment. Do you like it when you call a business and they just take your name and number, saying someone will call you back? It is sort of frustrating, right? You were ready and concentrated on setting that appointment, only to be told that someone will call you later. The problem is, later often never comes. If you are like most people, you will just pick up the phone book or Google another company.

Your customers are no different. There is no time like the present to set the appointment.

The first part of lead tracking begins with getting the information at the time of the very first contact. The first part of the sale begins by setting an appointment. Get them while they are buying!

Are You Stifling Your Salespeople
Through Tracking Requirements?

"Why do my salespeople refuse to use my CRM?"

Straight off the cuff, show your salespeople the value and benefits for them to use your CRM, and you'll have salespeople who use it! Do you have a Salespeople's CRM, or do you have a system that just requires extra work with no benefits?

In talking with different business owners, sales managers, and salespeople in regards to the implementation of CRMs or tracking systems, one common feedback is that they cannot get salesperson "buy in". In fact, they meet up with salespeople having an absolute disdain for CRM tracking systems.

Hearing this common theme, I have deduced two major issues: 1) the salesperson feels like every move is being watched, and 2) the salesperson does not recognize the value in why you want him/her to "buy into" the tracking system.

We all know that salespeople are salespeople for a few reasons, but one main reason is because they want to be their own boss. They are those "free spirits" in so many ways, especially those salespeople who are being paid straight commissions. They do not want to be tied down! They are moved by the possibility of getting on to the next sale, not by keeping immaculate notes. Most of them are not really interested in being tracked and having every call, correspondence, or move monitored. They feel squelched and almost kept under a thumb, so to speak.

Their feelings are not unsubstantiated. Well, sometimes they are, but think about this! We are living in a different world, and some people have gotten so caught up in technology and the methodology, that sales as they were are being forgotten, and the whole picture is not being seen. Salespeople are not being allowed to do what they do best: sell!

> *S*alespeople are not being allowed to do what they do best: sell!

Companies are implementing expensive and complicated systems and, understandably, expect their people to use it. A sales manager is expected to report specific data to the owners, and the only way they can get that data is through the cooperation of the salespeople. The salespeople, however, see this only as something that requires a lot more of their time each day. They not only lose precious time, but also lose their good attitudes and take on the frustration of delivering just because they have to, or they don't use it and then end up being harped on for not keeping the records up to date.

So why is this such a big conflict? Business owners know that tracking will increase revenues, but not everyone recognizes this. It is up to business owner to show their people how the system will make them real money! Show your salespeople a system that will make them more money, and they'll be all over it! Make sure that whatever system you are using and the information you are requiring of your salespeople is indeed providing an easier and faster path to sales, and will be of value to them when they put it to use!

The perceived value to the salesperson has to be there in order for them to use it. Don't worry about the little bells and whistles in a system that are not necessarily money-makers; just provide a simple system that your people can get going on easily and quickly. If you get your people going on a system that is simple, yet provides the necessary information they need to grow sales, it will no longer be an issue to get them to use a tracking system. A good salesperson will recognize the benefit. In fact, those good salespeople are kind of like a bunch of mini businesses right within your business – they want to follow the cash, and that's their main concern. Let them do that in a way that benefits them, which in turn will benefit you and the company.

As an aside, I recently asked one salesperson why he likes my particular tracking system, Profit Finder Pro Software, and his response was, "I like it because I know that when I go out on a sales call, I'm going to get the sale. They set me up with leads I can sell." Okay, that is his perception. Works for him, works for the business. In fact, going on a sales call knowing you're going to sell is a very, very good thing and works well for everyone.

Another salesperson I recently asked said he really liked that his system synced through to his phone since he spends most of his time on the road. Yes, very handy. Remember that salespeople do not like being tied to their desks.

It is true that winners know their numbers, yes, especially the best and most successful salespeople. Just make sure those numbers mean something. Provide a simple system that will work for them, yet will provide the numbers you need to make adjustments in your marketing, lead assignment, and sales training. You will all benefit. It's a win-win situation.

Who Should Be In Charge of Choosing the CRM Tracking System?

I'll answer that with a question. Who cares the most about the business? That person is exactly the one who should be in charge of choosing a CRM or lead, sales, and marketing tracking system.

There are others in the business who really care about the business, but no one cares about the bottom line as much as the owner(s). Most people do not really even understand everything that goes into determining the bottom line of business, so when a tracking system can make such a powerful impact on the company revenues and profitable growth, it only makes sense to have that decision come from the top and work its way down through the entire system. Let there be no mistaken understanding in this.

A lead, sales, and marketing tracking system should be chosen by the owner, and instituted as a part of company expectations, especially for those sales reps who are being provided company leads.

Owners are pretty clear on the bottom line, and that is why they are much more objective when looking at systems. If it does not help the bottom line, move on to examining the next.

CRM systems are a dime a dozen. Google CRM and you will find millions of results. Google something more inclusive such as *lead sales and marketing tracking software* and you will get fewer results, still in the millions, but closer to the type of tracking system you will want to focus on. It is a big, responsible job to find a system that will give you what you need to be able to keep an eye on the profit points of business.

Tracking does not have to be complicated to be effective. In fact, it can be rather simple. There are some huge CRM systems out there, and there are some simple CRMs. There are some very nice systems out there, and some with very nice possibilities when additional programming is done. Put it all in perspective, and choose one that fits you. Someone who needs the gigantic system with features and functions to serve millions of people does not need the same one as a small business with a smaller team. It works the same way with other software. If you are designing kitchens and bathrooms, you do not need the same CAD software programs used for drawing airports and shopping centers.

> *Tracking does not have to be complicated to be effective.*

Do not get caught up in the bells and whistles with all the millions of things a software can do. Your people will not use it; it adds complication. In fact, with our Profit Finder Pro software, we make a deliberate attempt to keep it simple so that people will use it. It becomes easy for "feature creep" to get in the way of the simple necessities, thus driving your sales and marketing people away from using it, and becoming a worthless investment of your time and money. Do not let "feature creep" distract you and get in the way of your real purpose of having a lead, sales, and marketing tracking software system.

Whatever system you choose, make sure that you are fully aware of its capabilities right from the time you "plug it in". How much programming will be required and at what cost to you? How much time will it take to set it up? How much training is required? What kind of support is available? What happens to the data if you do not continue with it at some point? What kind of contracts are required?

And most importantly, in order for your software to be a tool that can be used to run and grow your business profitably, at a minimum it should give you the numbers as have been spelled out in this book. There are some systems that include lead count and lead cost, but without a large investment in extra programming, they probably do not tie those leads to the sales reps, the service provided, and the cost of getting a sale by sales rep and lead source.

Many of the systems are empty shells waiting to be programmed. Just be sure you know what you are getting compared to what you need. Make absolutely sure with your own eyes that the numbers are there, because I am here to tell you, as of the time this book was printed, there is not one system we have found that included the very numbers we needed to grow our business; that is why we had to create one ourselves. We needed those numbers. And so do you.

Business owners, it's up to you to find a system that will help your sales and marketing people shine!

Winners know their numbers. Make sure you know yours.

Questions for Your Business:

1. How many leads do you need to reach your company or personal goal?
2. What kind of action are you taking to make sure you get that number of leads?
3. What steps can you take to make sure your appointment setting process "grabs the customer" while they're on the phone?
4. What type of system have you set up for your salespeople that allows them to do what they do best, while at the same time enables them to be efficient in tracking their customer information, appointments, and sales cycle, and being able to use that information to their benefit in sales and generating more revenues?
5. In your business, who is in charge of setting up systems and choosing a CRM that focuses on the very numbers a business owner needs in order to grow revenues?
6. Winners Know Their Numbers. Do you? If you have a system in place, does it provide the numbers and information that has been spoken of in these chapters? If not, what are you waiting for?

NOTES

Chapter 13

Meanwhile, Back on the Farm...

Come with me to the farm for a bit. I want to give you a little insight into the tracking of a farmer.

Our farm, Pioneer Lane Farm, was straight west of Minneapolis, Minnesota, about forty miles. It was an historical site in Minnesota because it was one of the few round barns left in the state. The barn was built in 1901, its diameter was 80 feet, and it was approximately 80 feet to the top of the cupola. There was an aisle with two rows of stanchions for the cows, and then a short row to the west side of the barn, with calf pens on both sides of the stanchions, two hay chutes, a straw chute, the silage chute from the silo, and then the milk house. The ground level walls were 8 feet high, and built by big rocks and boulders hauled in from the area. The second level was a huge open hayloft (with a rope swing that hung from the rafters of the cupola). That barn could be seen from miles across the countryside. It was unique, a landmark, and it was not unusual for people to stop to take pictures or ask to step in to see it.

Going into the barn, you would step into the cool, damp milk house with a real low ceiling. A weight hung on the door to keep it from sticking open, because the room needed to remain cool. There was a big stock tank sunk into the floor, and it had a trickle of cold well water running into it to cool the milk cans until the milkman came each morning to pick them up to haul to the creamery. This is the way it was until after I graduated from high school. Shortly thereafter, they added an extension to the milking parlor and switched to pipeline milking where the milk went directly from the cows into the pipe system and then to the cooled milk tank. The milkman then only needed to hook a hose to the bulk tank and empty it into his big milk truck that way. That was much easier than the backbreaking job of hauling the heavy cans!

From the milk house it was just a step into the barn. The smell of the sweet hay would fill your senses, and sometimes you could see the dust in the air if hay had recently been dropped from the hayloft.

The barn was usually a pretty quiet and calm place, with the noises of the milkers quietly chuffing in the background while contented cows chewed on hay, silage, or grain. The radio that hung from the ceiling was usually tuned into NPR or some soft, calm music station. Supposedly this helped keep the cows calm, and calm cows milked better.

Beginning at 5:30 twice a day, Dad and the others would be going about their jobs – washing, milking, feeding, and cleaning. It was a routine, two times a day, day after day, week after week, month after month, year after year. The cows were milked in the same order, every time, every day. The repetition was so precise, and the schedule so consistent, that one could almost set a clock to it.

If you would look around and pay close attention, you'd notice certain things about the barn. For example, there were cardboard tags hanging from a wire above every cow's stanchion with numbers written, scratched out, and written again. On that tag was the cow's name and the weight of grain to give for each feeding. Sometimes the cow would get the same weight both in the morning and the afternoon, but sometimes it was different. The amount of grain was determined by the pounds of milk the cow produced. If it was a high-producing cow, the weight of grain would be higher than it would be for the lower producing cows. At feeding time, we would push the feed cart with a scale attached, fill the pail with grain, and then weigh it to make sure we were feeding each cow the proper amount.

Dad had a 100% registered Guernsey Dairy herd for most of his farming career. Guernseys came to the United States around 1840 from Guernsey Island, a little island off France in the English Channel. This breed of cow is known for its high-butterfat and high-protein milk with a high concentration of beta carotene. Beta carotene is needed by our bodies to convert into Vitamin A, which we use for healthy skin, a healthy immune system, and good eye health and vision.

By nature, Guernseys have a gentle disposition. They are a medium-sized animal and are able to produce a high quality milk while eating up to 30% less feed per pound of milk produced than breeds that are of a larger build.

In addition to that, they typically calve more often, and begin calving at a younger age than other breeds.

Already way back in the late 1870s, people understood how important it was to have a purebred herd and know the lineage of each cow or sire. It was important because if your herd was all sired by the same bull, and the herd breeds with offspring of the same line/family, eventually you end up with a weakened herd. Inbreeding works the same way in cattle as it does in human genetics, and would be very similar to relatives inbreeding for offspring, and then those offspring continuing to reproduce with the offspring of those close relatives.

The sheer numbers of keeping a large enough herd with a large enough variety of bulls and cows from different family lines in order to keep a strong gene pool was impossible for any single person or even a small community of people. That is exactly why the pedigrees and the genealogical lineage of the cattle were so important. Guernsey farmers all around the United States were willing to keep and share this information, because it was in the best interest of all of them to keep a strong herd.

When registering a bull or heifer, Dad would give its name, the names of its dam and sire, and its date of birth. He also had to provide the milk tester's records: the report of the butterfat percentage, the number of pounds the cow produced, when they last calved, what they delivered (male or female), and the health records. The records of all these animals were updated every now and then.

Artificial insemination has been used for many years in building strong cattle herds, and before breeding any cows, Dad would study the American Guernsey Breeding Journal for both National and Minnesota Breeder's Associations to find a good bull to sire any heifer or calf. If it was a heifer that was being bred for the first time, when reading the pedigrees, he would consider the size of the sire, because if the calf was too large for the size of the heifer, it could make a real difficult birth and, in worse cases, the heifer could even die. In researching the pedigrees, though, a good body type and the milk production of the sire's mother were the biggest attributes he considered.

A dairy farmer's income depends on having enough milking cows at any given time, and so everything that goes on with the cows and the heifers becomes very systematic. Specific steps are taken simply because it is part of the equation for running a successful dairy farm.

For those of you who are not familiar with the terms, when a cow gives birth to a calf, that calf is either female or male. Females are called heifers, and males are called bulls. Once a heifer gives birth to a calf, it becomes a cow. A bull is used for breeding, unless it is castrated, in which case it becomes a steer. A steer's primary purpose is to be fattened and raised as beef cattle. Beef cattle can be steer, cow, or heifer that is being fattened for its beef. To set the record straight, there are no boy cows! I say this half laughing and half serious because there really were those who we farm kids termed "city slickers" that asked how to tell the difference between a boy cow and a girl cow.

From the moment of birth, the life from being just a heifer to becoming a cow is measured. A heifer is not supposed to give birth before two years. That meant at 15 months they could be bred, and then they would freshen around two years. Freshen means the cow has given birth and becomes a milk-producing cow.

Remember I said that Guernseys are able to calve more often than other breeds? Around sixty days (or a minimum of forty-five days) after having given birth a cow could be bred again. The date they freshened was kept track of, so any time after forty-five days we would start to watch the cow's behavior to see when it would be time to call the breeder.

During the approximate nine month period while expecting a calf, a cow still milks, but then around two months before calving, the cow is "dried up", which means not milked. Generally speaking, the average lactation or milking year of a cow is 305 days. Dad usually timed breeding so that the majority of the cows were "dried up" late in the summer and early fall. By late fall we were milking full blast again with large milk production and lots of calves to take care of... after the harvest was done! It was also timed this way for health reasons for the calves. Bugs were at a minimum in the winter, which made the calf pens much healthier.

A calf got the mother's new milk, colostrum, which was full of nutrients and antibodies for the first three days after birth. After a couple days, the colostrum was gone, and the cow was producing regular milk. At that time, the calf would get any cow's milk, not necessarily just from its mother, until it was weaned from milk at 42 days.

Are you starting to see all the tracking that has gone on in the whole process of selecting sires and breeding for calves, and why it was important? As you continue to read, you will clearly understand why my dad had a pile of ledgers on his desk, the everlasting, money-making "eyesore" in one corner of the house!

I mentioned earlier that the genetics of cattle works the same way as humans and other species. The same holds true for diet. Basically, you are what you eat! If you eat junk food, you don't feel as good, you don't perform as well, and you just do not operate at prime. If you eat healthy food, you feel much better, your body functions better and overall, things are just better. It works the same way with the cows!

There was a measured method for making food for the cows. When we mixed grain for feed, we had to weigh all the ingredients. Corn, oats, vitamins, minerals, soybean meal for protein, salt, and beet pulp from the Red River Valley for fiber and flavor. We mixed those proportions according to the feed company recommendations. They would take our feed samples and analyze them. Then they would also test the alfalfa and the corn silage to tell us what vitamins and minerals to add to the mixed feed.

This made a difference in the yield of milk. If balanced properly, the cows would breed on time and produce more milk. And they would look better, healthier. Their coat would have a nice sheen, and the look in their eyes was clearer.

The heifers did not get a grain mixture because they were not producing milk yet. Their diet was alfalfa and corn silage, and we'd set out salt blocks for them to lick. The salt block gave minerals they were not getting from the alfalfa and corn silage.

The beef cattle (steers) would graze in the pastures in the spring, summer, and fall, and then be fed hay and silage during the winter. When they were reaching the point where they were close to butchering time, they were fed grain to add the finishing touch and weight for the perfect table beef. We did not keep many beef cattle, just enough for our own use. (By the way, if you like meat and you have not had home-grown, non-GMO, non-antibiotic fed beef, you have not lived!)

Dad did not keep bulls around our place since they were not used as sires for his herd. When they were born, he would sell them to the stockyards at a rather young age for veal. There was at least one time when one of our bulls that came from a very good lineage was sold at the Guernsey Association auction as a sire for another farmer's herds. That same bull was consequently sold by that farmer to one of the breeding companies to be used for artificial insemination.

The milk tester would come every month and set up his little table in the middle of the barn aisle. It was full of test tubes standing in a tray. He would weigh the milk and get samples to send in to test the amount of butterfat. Based on those results each month, Dad would get back a report for the feed system for each cow; how much and what kind of food. Then he would go scratch out and update the previous notes hanging above each cow's stanchion with the recommended weight of grain for each cow. The goal was to get as much production volume, protein content, and butterfat as possible because the creamery paid for volume, protein content, and butterfat.

The typical lifespan of a cow was anywhere from five to eight years, and each cow averaged about three calves.

It was hard for Dad to go on vacation or be away during milking time because he was rightfully very concerned about the cows' health. Cows are very sensitive to being over-milked. And over-milking is easy to do if you are not familiar with the individual cows. If cows are over-milked, they often develop mastitis, which is a bad health condition that has to be cured with antibiotics. During that time period the milk cannot be sold and the cow generally is not nearly as productive for the rest of that lactation period. In really bad cases, some cows may never totally recover, which would be a terrible loss and big price to pay for taking time off.

Farmers have always been and continue to be dependent on the weather. They put a lot of faith, hope, and trust that the weather will be good for them to plant and harvest their crops; after all, their livelihood depends on the weather! Risk takers, every one of them!

The type of seed used for different crops depends on the season and where you live in the country. There is a certain window of time for growing conditions (weather) for different seeds. If you do not have 105 days as some crops require, you might have to switch to an earlier maturity seed. Farmers would rather have a longer maturity because the shorter a maturity, the lower the yield. That's why farmers keep such an eye on the sky, and are so antsy to get in the fields in the spring. Every day can make a big difference in the end crop yield.

In the winter, the seed catalogs come. It has always been a wonder how the seed companies come up with such great photos and descriptions of their products. Maybe the pictures helped make up for all the technical terms which are gobbledy gook to most of us but made perfect sense to the farmers, including my dad. I will not bore you to death with the details, but based on a seed's yield expectations, days required from planting to harvest, resistance to disease and pests, and several other bits and pieces of information, including consulting his copy of The Old Farmer's Almanac (hey, you need to get the odds in your favor as much as possible!), the seed order was made.

There was a definite system for what was planted in each field and the crop rotation each year. The condition of the soil depends a lot on the rotation of the crops, so if you keep using and renewing the soil the way it should be, you will get a much better crop. If you plant corn year after year after year in the same field, it will deplete the soil of certain nutrients, and your corn crop will eventually fail. If you rotate, the other crops will replenish the soil with missing nutrients, break up the disease cycles that come with some crops, lessen the need for pesticides, and make the soil rich again.

We planted oats, corn, alfalfa, soybeans, wheat, barley and sorghum. Some years we did not do all of them, but for sure oats, corn, alfalfa, and soybeans.

Before planting crops, the soil conditions had to be right for each one in order for the seeds to germinate and break through the surface as quickly as they should. They paid attention to the temperature, the moisture, and the nutrients. Ideally, the temperature of the soil should have been around 50 F, but in reality, if there was a delayed spring, there were times when we just had to get the crops in once the fields were not solid muck.

The soil was tested some years, especially when moisture content was a concern. Soil testing also could help to determine how much fertilizer to use and more. When weeds were a concern, a determination needed to be made to come up with precisely the correct herbicide blend to use, as well as the precise amount. It was important to watch the weather before putting down herbicides so the rain would not wash it away. Timing was important for everything that went down in the fields.

The first crop we planted in the spring was oats because they liked cooler weather. In fact, it would be ideal if the oats froze after coming up because then there would be a bumper crop. When there was a little freeze, the oats would tiller, or grow additional branches and the yield would be better.

Alfalfa (hay) was seeded in with the oats a year before we would get an alfalfa crop from that field. The oats or wheat crop would come up that year and we would harvest that, but at the same time, the alfalfa was growing a good root system below. The wheat or oats had provided a nice shelter from the weeds taking over, and allowed the alfalfa seedlings to grow in peace. Then the following three years, that alfalfa would grow and be harvested from the same field. After the third year, we plowed it up and planted corn in that field the following year because the alfalfa would have fixed the nitrogen, and corn uses a lot of nitrogen for growth. The fifth year, soy beans were planted because soy beans also fix the nitrogen and make the soil ready for corn again the next year. Then the oats and alfalfa and would be rotated.

Alfalfa was the hardest to harvest because we were so dependent on the weather to be nice for a number of consecutive days. The alfalfa needed to be baled just before it started to bloom because the protein percentage was higher. But the weather forecast also needed to be good so that the alfalfa could be cut and dried before it was baled. First we cut and crushed it, splitting the stems so moisture could get out. Then after it dried we raked it into rows that the baler could pick up, and then baled it. In order to prevent mold, or even worse, a combustion fire hazard, we could not put damp alfalfa in a barn hayloft. (Tightly-packed damp or wet hay is a great growing place for organisms, and that activity causes heat, which could cause a combustion fire.)

Dad needed to make absolutely certain that the cows had plenty of quality hay and feed in order to have the proper ingredients for them to produce the best quality and largest quantity of milk as possible. The better those numbers were, the better the balance was in the checkbook! The hay baler had a counter that let him know how many bales were made that day, which he was able to use for a bunch of different data:

1. How many bales of hay were made per acre of land per crop (there were three crops per year).
2. Obviously he could total the three crops and know how many bales of hay an acre of land produced for the year.
3. Finally, knowing how much was eaten by the cattle the prior year would let him know how many acres of land needed to be planted into alfalfa the next year.

117

Oats and beans were tracked by bushels. Dad's bins held a certain volume, so in order to know how many bushels he had, he would just look to see how full the bins were, how far up the wall they went, at the end of harvest.

Part of Dad's income was from selling the "cash crops" which were soybeans and any excess corn and oats that were not used for feed. The selling needed to happen prior to harvest simply to make room for the current year's crop. The exact timing for selling the cash crops depended on when the price was right, the need for cash, or other factors. He listened to the grain market reports for the price of corn and soybeans in the Chicago Commodities every day, and then when the time was right, he'd sell.

As a side note, one year the government was paying farmers to not grow corn, the Set-Aside Program. Dad asked one of my brothers what he thought about it, and my brother figured that since at least 25 to 30% of corn was not going to be grown that year, the price would go up considerably. Dad grew corn, the price did go up, and he did well on that decision.

The corn was harvested in two parts, and for two purposes. Corn silage was a main part of the cattle's diet, so the silos had to be filled with enough chopped silage to last the year. Again, this was another process that was more than just chopping the corn stalks and blowing it into the silo. It was very precise, because the silage would need to go through a fermentation process. Depending on how it fermented, the cows would or would not eat it as willingly.

In order for it to ferment properly, the corn silage needed to be harvested at the right moisture (about 70%) and maturity for optimum nutrients. This period of time was about a week, so when it was ready, they needed to act fast to get it chopped and blown into the silo. Usually Dad or one of the boys could tell when it was ready because the corn kernels would sink about halfway down to the black level. If there was a question, they could bring a sample to the mill in town, and the guys at the mill would test it for moisture content.

Already before harvest, the machinery had been gotten ready to go and was waiting in the machine shed, so once we got the word that the corn was ready, there would be no waiting on machines. The corn chopper was set to chop the corn a certain size, maybe 1 inch pieces, to make for easier digestion for the cows.

We younger kids would be in the silo tramping down the silage as it came down the chute, as an older brother would direct the path of the chute in our old silo. In the new one, it was automated. If the silage had gotten too dry or below 70% content, another person would be standing there with a hose, spraying the silage as it was blown in.

The fermentation process would begin right away, and within about 72 hours the oxygen supply in the silo was depleted, so it became a dangerous place to be. That is why we had to get it filled, packed, and get out of there as quickly as possible.

After filling silos, the rest of the corn fields were used for the cobs and kernels of corn itself. During the winter those cobs with the kernels attached would be ground in with the feed for the cows. At the end of the season, any leftover corn would be emptied from the corn cribs, shelled, sold in order to make room for the fresh crop coming in.

Corn shelling time was a really busy time on our farm! There was a team of corn shellers (a group of big, huge men), that would come with their machinery. We used their machines and our muscle power to empty the corn cribs. They would come early in the morning, and stay until dark, and this lasted a few days. Looking back, it really was like the old harvest times you read about in novels; a team would come and work to get it done and then move on to the next farm. They worked with us and ate with us at our dining room table for dinner, supper, and coffee lunch breaks, and then hustled back out to continue the shelling.

Once the cribs were empty, Dad could harvest the new corn. This was a time when we would all help again. Someone would drive the full wagons to the corn crib, and a couple others would be there with the forks to pull it into the elevator, and then the empty wagon would be taken out to the field again to trade with the next wagon which was probably already full. This happened over and over and over again for the next few days until the corn was all picked and the cribs were full.

119

Then there were the soy beans. These were strictly a cash crop. They had to be harvested at the right time, too. Dad could do his own inspection by picking a few pods and chewing the beans. If they were too chewy, they were still too wet. If it seemed they were close to done, then he could bring a sample to the mill for testing. If all was good, then the harvest would begin. There were times that if the weather forecast was not looking good, but the beans were close to ready, we would have to harvest them early. Since they were not quite dry enough, they would have to be put in bins with a dryer. Of course, it was preferable if the weather would cooperate long enough for the crop to mature and be taken in when it was ready, because it took a lot of electricity and fuel to run the dryer on those huge bins, and ended up being quite costly.

As kids we had so many places to roam and play on the acres of land. There were not have too many places we could not go...except the granary with the oats and beans. Dad did not want us to play in there. You know how kids are; somehow they know how to throw the beans and scatter them everywhere but where they should be. Yes, looking back, I see that. But have you ever fallen back into a humongous pile of soybeans? The soft, cool, smooth surface of the beans and the light, sweet smell... We could not resist. If you knew the feel and smell, you would not be able to resist either. In fact, we would even bring our dolls and play house for hours in the soybean bin. Or sometimes we would just go in there with a comic book and read away the afternoon by the window near the top of the pile. It was something so indescribably neat that I even had to bring my friends in there from time to time. It was not too often that we got caught doing this, but if so, we certainly got the marching orders out of there.

There was time for plenty of fun on the farm, too. The boys did their hunting, fishing, trapping, monkeying around with their go-carts, dirt bikes, motorcycles, or snowmobiles. They, along with their friends, built elaborate hay forts and mazes that were held up with planks of wood so the hay above would not collapse. Then they would come get us and we would have to go try to find their forts and follow the mazes to try catch them. Crazy fun stuff! They had all kinds of hidden coves, trapdoors, and really, when I think back on it, this ended up being great practice for home design and construction.

After chores in the summer, they would head out to the cabin to swim, or in the winter they would ice-fish on a Saturday. I don't know what all they did, but we did not have a lot of bored people sitting around waiting to be entertained.

Part of the "fun" was also an important part of keeping clean food for the cattle. A hayloft is a great place for starlings and pigeons, both of which can take over with their population, become a nuisance, a real health hazard, and be destructive. They leave their droppings all over the hay, and the disease they may carry can be transferred on to the cows, which carries right down the food chain to contaminated food and higher prices for the consumer. As youngsters, we learned how to handle bb guns, and it was okay for us to get rid of them when we saw them in the hayloft.

Speaking of the food chain and prices, nowadays Monsanto and GMOs are all over the news, in health magazines, and all over the place. I'm not sure when all of it initially started, but this was exactly what the farmers were resisting already way back in the late 70s or early 80s! Now we have seen the domino effect, and only now is when the public starts hollering, about forty years after it has gotten such a strong foothold throughout the food system.

I have gone over a lot of explanation from the tracking that happens and was necessary in running our farm as a business, but I have not even mentioned what all went on inside the house yet! That is another whole story in and of itself, and without this part of the story, the farm business would not have functioned.

Many of you have perhaps read Napoleon Hill's books on the Secrets of Success. A big part of that speaks about having a purpose behind the goal for success. Dad's purpose, I believe, was driven because of his desire to provide a nice life for his wife and family. In return for that nice life, he was willing to give of himself day in and day out. The same held true for Mom. Her purpose and satisfaction in this life came from being a help and support for her husband, as well as to take care of and provide for the needs inside the home. They worked as a team, each in their areas of expertise, in order to provide a nice life and home for each other and their family.

Mom was very organized. She did not necessarily track a lot of things, per se, but she had definite systems in place for everyone and everything. Each one of us kids had specific chores to do, and for the most part, the girls worked in the house, unless they preferred to be out in the barn (as one of my sisters did). During harvest or haying, the girls would pitch in, too. We all spent times helping out here or there in the barn, but for the most part, it was Dad, the boys and one sister that did the outside work.

First of all, housework on a farm is not peaches and cream. It is continuous work, just like the outside work. If you wanted a house that did not smell like the barn, you had to constantly be scrubbing and cleaning. Well, my mom was a city girl, and the last thing she wanted was for her house to smell! So, we eight girls were lucky she had the patience and determination to teach us the lifelong skills of keeping a house clean and life organized.

I only recognize the huge work load as I look back, though. In fact, many times after reaching adulthood I have marveled and wondered how Mom did it! It was amazing to me that with as much going on as there was, the home was calm, and it was a good life. We worked hard, plus we had plenty time for play, fun, and hobbies. Part of this is because Mom was so organized and had all her systems in place in order for the household to run smoothly.

Our 1917 house was a Sears Roebuck home, probably the Chelsea model, if you are familiar with Sears Roebuck homes. Basically, the person would pick a house plan from a catalog, make changes to the blueprint as desired, and then Sears would get together all the lumber, precut it and send that along with all the supplies, down to the nails. (See a picture of our house and farm at www.finnishcheese.com). It was one of those stately, huge homes with a lot of beautiful oak woodwork, thick baseboards and crown moulding, columns between the rooms, and built-in buffets and bookshelves, with heavy spider-key doors, some of them having beveled mirrors or glass. The floors were maple throughout, and the house had three stories plus a basement. Needless to say, there was a lot of dusting and cleaning to do!

Every morning when we woke up, we knew what to wear because our clothes had been laid out the night before. This was a habit Mom had us start when we began school. I am sure it was so that no one would be held up in the morning because they could not decide what to wear or because they could not find matching socks or something else that would put a crimp in starting the day. We also had home clothes, school clothes and church clothes. There was a distinct difference, which made the choice of what we were wearing each day a little easier. To this day, I lay out my clothes the night before. Some habits just stick.

In the afternoon, when we came home from school there was a piece of paper on the kitchen table listing the chores we each had to do that day. It was up to us as to when we did them, but they all had to be done before going to sleep that night. The sooner we got done with our little checklist, the sooner we could get on with other fun things like playing outside, reading, homework, or whatever else we had going on.

The chores would rotate from age to age, or week to week. Already as soon as we were able to take the toys from the toy box and make a mess, we were old enough to pick them up and put them back. Around age 4 or 5, we would start emptying the dishwasher or clearing the table. As we got older, we would rotate between putting clothes away, washing the kettles and counters, sweeping, vacuuming, dusting, baking, washing floors, even taking care of the little kids, playing with them and keeping them happy, occupied and out of trouble. Whatever job we had, it was scheduled and rotated.

I'm telling you, my mom loved checklists. Of course, as kids we had a love/hate relationship with those lists as we looked to see what we had to do each day, but oh what a happy thing to cross the jobs off as we finished them! As much as it was kind of annoying as a kid sometimes, checklists are something that also became a habit and daily part of my life. In college I lived by my list. When I was a classroom teacher and then elementary school principal, I always had a checklist of the day's things to accomplish. When I go to the office now, the first thing I look at is my daily task list. Crossing things off is still just as much fun, and almost done with a flair!

Mondays were always the big washing day, but of course with so many people there were loads of laundry to wash every day except Sundays. Mom loved washing, hanging wet clothes on the line outside, folding and ironing clothes, so we kids did not do much of that. Besides that, she did not like dingy clothes and was quite particular about what went in each load and the temperatures at which they were washed– whites with whites, towels with towels, barn clothes in this pile, and so on. That meant every Monday after school, there were clean clothes to put away. There were labeled baskets on a shelf above the washer and dryer that held all the folded clothes, and whoever had that job needed to put all those away.

Tuesdays were piano lessons, so other than dishes and sweeping the entry or vacuuming the floors, it was a slim day for other chores.

Wednesdays were always Bible class, so again, not too many chores other than dishes, sweeping and picking up.

Thursdays we would clean the upstairs. That meant going through every room, dusting everything, washing mirrors, windows, vacuuming everywhere including the closets and under the beds, scrubbing the bathroom from top to bottom, and just doing an overall thorough cleaning.

Fridays we cleaned the downstairs, the main floor. Same thing. Dust, polish, vacuum under, above and around everything, including under the couch cushions and moving all the chairs and lamp tables to get under every week. Wood floors were scrubbed by hand.

Saturdays were always a baking and deep-cleaning day. We each had our own chores again: clean the basement, clean the attic, scrub the sauna, and bake from sun up to sun down. And then Saturday evenings, we always had company over, and fresh-baked goodies to serve them for coffee lunch. Families used to visit as families a lot back then, and my parents were entertainers. They loved having company over.

Sundays were always reserved for church, visiting, and relaxing. We always set the table and ate our meals together in the dining room, and on Sundays we usually pulled out the linens and china, and more often than not, we had dinner visitors.

Mom was an excellent cook and especially loved baking. I have yet to find caramel rolls as good as hers. She was very particular about following recipes in a certain way, and took impeccable notes. If she changed the way she made something, she notated it. That way, when we were learning how to bake, all she had to do was tell us to pay close attention to the recipe, and always read through it first. On each recipe card is the name of the person who gave her the recipe, so in a way, her recipe boxes are a walk down Memory Lane. Even now when I go home, I still flip through recipes, and lots of memories of all those old family friends come to mind. I doubt she had that in mind when she wrote them, but it ended up being a special side benefit.

Around our place, like most farm families, we canned beans, pickles, tomatoes, beets from the garden, froze corn from our fields and apples from our orchard every year. When Mom canned, she always kept track of how many quarts or pints we made. Then when the next season came, she would send someone down to the fruit cellar to count what was left and then she would adjust how much was canned that year. The same held true for freezing corn and apples.

Mom kept really good records for many different things. She had a box on a shelf in the laundry room that was full of recipe cards and dividers. In there she wrote down all the immunization records and special dates or other things to remember for each child. For special occasions such as baptisms, graduations, showers, weddings, she would keep track of what was on the menu, quantity made, and how many people were served. Then when she planned an event for the next child, there was a basis to make her plans.

Mom was not one for keeping a lot of extra stuff around, including clothes that did not fit or were not worn. We lived in Minnesota, a land of distinct seasons, so spring and fall were perfect times to do what we called Spring and Fall Cleaning! Along with vacuuming every ceiling and wall, washing all the woodwork (of which we had A LOT), with vinegar water, washing and waxing the wood floors, and cleaning all the windows, we also went through every drawer and closet. Each of us had a trunk for our off-season clothes and garment bags for the hanging dress clothes in the attic. Mom would have us try on everything, and if it was something that did not fit, it was either passed on to the next child, stuck in a pile for her and her bosom friend Marian's garage sale, or stuck in a pile to drop off at Goodwill, Salvation Army, or some other donation place. She did not usually keep things around for another child to grow into because we would end up with too much stuff sitting around. Also by the time it would fit the next child a couple years later, the styles had changed. Besides that, she loved shopping!

One thing we learned very quickly *not* to say around home was, 'I'm bored.' If we did, it would probably take about two seconds flat to find a chore for the bored one. Mom did tell us a time or two that, "If you are bored, you must be a boring person!" Needless to say, we were not necessarily interested in being boring (and wanted another chore even less), so we found all kinds of things to keep us entertained, including some pretty fun hobbies.

Homework for all of us was certainly not an all-evening affair like you hear about today. Once we finished our chores, it was up to us to get our school work done. If we got stuck, we would ask an older sister or brother, unless it was something to do with History or Geography. Then we would ask Dad! He was and still is a real history buff. He loved the encyclopedias, and when we would ask a question, he would suggest pulling that out. I think all of us got lost more than once in the encyclopedias! (Later on Mom and Dad came to know all about Google, too! For some reason it still makes me chuckle to hear the over-80s people say, 'Google it.')

Neither Mom nor Dad were helicopter parents that hovered over every paper we wrote or project we did; however, they certainly wanted us to do well, and expected that we would do our best. In fact, at report card time, before even opening the report card, they would ask, 'Did you do your best?' That was what mattered most. They cared about our schooling, but it was our responsibility to get as much out of it as we could. Bringing home report cards and having them smile and say, 'Nice job' was all we needed to keep us motivated and going.

All of us girls and a couple of the boys took piano lessons, so there was always someone plunking on the piano in the foyer. Starting with the youngest first, we had a specific time to practice every day after school, and we would set the timer on the oven for however long we were supposed to practice. See? We even had to track our piano practicing! The main reason for that was so that the teacher could see whether or not we were progressing at a rate proportionate to our practicing.

Both Mom and Dad instilled a love of reading in each one of us by their example. Every evening, Mom would read to the little kids before bed. It was a good way to relax and quiet down for the night, and a chance to all sit together, visit, and just be still. Even as a high-schooler, I would bring my homework to the dining room table to sit there and work on it while half an ear was tuned into whatever story she was reading to the little kids. This was always a nice way to wind down the day.

On the farm, our lives revolved around the seasons, each of which held its own duties and chores in the barn, in the fields, and in the house. At the end of harvest, the machinery would all go back to the machine shed for Dad to work on and maintain during the quieter winter months. The extra hustle and bustle of the summer and fall season slowed down in the house, too, and more hand crafts and hobbies started up again.

It was a continuous circle. The seasons, the work, the life.

Through it all, we grew up a family. Each of us kids eventually left home one by one to follow our dreams and make our ways in the world, but we all share that same connection which was built on the same foundations and teachings of life, how we are to live, the love and strong ties of family, home, and the good life on the farm. And this is where our story began.

Author's Note: In writing this last chapter, I talked to Dad and each of my siblings to get feedback about the kinds of tracking we did on the farm. It ended up being quite nostalgic, in a sense, as we traveled down Memory Lane. Mom would have enjoyed sharing these memories, too.

About the Author

Susan Raisanen, President of Profit Pro CRM, is a lead, sales, and marketing tracking expert. She not only sells a software system she and her brothers developed for their own businesses, but is also a speaker who has held many seminars and continuously provides online seminars that show how tracking and taking action on certain elements of sales and marketing can make all the difference between a business thriving or barely surviving.

Susan is the tenth of fifteen children. Their family grew up in a small farming community just west of Minneapolis, MN. Family has always been important for her, and she feels that the strong sense of roots, love, and belonging have allowed her to do the things she has done. Going home is always just as sweet.

Susan is a teacher by profession, and most of her students were in the sixth and seventh grades. After teaching for seven years, she was an elementary school principal for another seven years before getting involved in small business. At that point, she was hooked on Small Business America, and there have been no regrets or turning back!

Music has been a big part of her (and her family's) life and, though she has dabbled with many instruments, her favorite is the piano. She is a church organist, and has been since she started accompanying the Sunday School at age 13. During college she worked in the music department, tutoring music students, and in the evenings had her own piano students as a means to pay for her college tuition.

Susan has had opportunities to travel the world, and even lived and taught overseas for a few years. According to her, the more she traveled, the smaller the world became, and although the cultures and societies are extremely different, people are pretty much the same at heart and have the same basic needs all over the world.

Outside of the office, Susan rarely has a dull moment. Being "bored" is not part of her vocabulary. She learned that if she were bored at home as a child, they were sure to be given a cleaning rag to cure it. She and her brothers and sisters always found plenty to keep busy.

An avid reader, Susan consumes everything she can about other successful leaders in life and business. She is a golfer and loves the outdoors, but also enjoys indoor hobbies such as beading or re-stringing old Mikimoto and other pearls.

Most of all, Susan is a people-person and loves spending time in the company of family and friends She adores her nieces and nephews, some of which are nearly her own age, and some of whom are still just babies. She believes that every person has their own story, and the people we meet along the way are what makes life so fun and interesting. She has dug deeply into the stories of her own family history and genealogy along both her mother and father's lines, and figures that some day when the time is right, she'll get started on a historical fiction series that she has mapped out.

Susan really enjoys what she does. Being able to show business owners and managers how to take a few simple steps in tracking and see it make such a huge difference in the direction of their businesses, and therefore their lives, gives her joy

About *Profit Finder Pro*
Software

Profit Finder Pro Software was developed as a result of the need for many of the numbers described in this book, and was created by small business owners for small business owners.

It is a lead, sales and marketing tracking CRM that allows a business owner or manager to keep an eye on the pulse of the key profit indicators in sales and marketing, while allowing sales people access to their customers and prospects from a desktop, smart phone or tablet at any given time. The scheduling part of the software is especially helpful for an office that has a human being taking incoming calls and setting appointments.

If you are a business owner or manager that spends money on marketing and distributes leads to sales representatives, this is of interest to you, especially if you want to run or grow your business profitably.

In order to schedule an online demonstration of the software, email *info@ProfitFinderPro.com* or call 1-800-972-6952. Tell them you read this book, and if you find the software is a good fit for your company, you will receive a special discount of 50% off the initial cost of setup, not including extra programming.

Put More Profit in your Pocket!

Cut the Fat, Waste and Frustration from your Sales and Marketing.

If you have been inspired to join the ranks of other successful business owners who have transformed their businesses through effective tracking, call **1-800-972-6952** or email *info@ProfitFinderPro* to set a time for an online consultation and review of software that could take away your troubles and get you on the path to greater profits. Be sure to mention the code: "I READ THE BOOK" for a 50% limited-time discount on setup if you decide that this is the solution for you! (Value approximately $250).

Made in the USA
San Bernardino, CA
07 February 2017